UNDERSTANDING THE ROOTS OF FASCISM

WALTER J. KRUECKL

UNDERSTANDING THE ROOTS OF FASCISM
Walter J. Krueckl

Copyright © 2014 by Walter J. Krueckl
978-0-9937991-0-5

Grove Street Publishing
Vancouver, B. C., Canada

Dedicated to all the victims of fascism.

ACKNOWLEDGEMENTS

Thanks to Ian (Douglas) Johnson for his editing skills and support. Thanks to my parents Helen and George Krueckl for their support and encouragement. I would also like to thank the following people for their help and inspiration: Taj (Paul) Tallalian, Zoe Namoe, Adi Gevins, Michael Bumblebee, Joyce Kaufman, Wayne Hatford, Robert Hunter, Jon Harris, Darcy Scan Clarke, Tim Holzworth, Dianne Stevenson, Ernie Gagnon, Cecile Scott, Pam Coren, and Marty Hill.

CONTENTS

FOREWORD

Having written this book on fascism in 1977, and not being able to find an outlet to publish it, I wrote a few articles on it, made a few speeches, and finally laid the manuscript aside. Then life happened, and years passed, then decades, all the while figuring if nothing else, I'd publish it later on in my life when I had the time to do it. Well, here I am retired with plenty time, and here is my book.

Although written when I was young and idealistic, the premise and thesis of this work stand firm. After much prodding from friends and family, I revisited the manuscript and realized it was just as relevant as ever and needed to be published. Even though so much has happened in our world since 1977, the fundamentals for the development of fascism remain the same.

In the mean time, there have been many dangerous developments that threaten our democracies and promote the rise of fascism. In response to terrorism in America, the Patriot's Act after 9:11 has eroded and undermined freedom of expression due to the resulting use of excessive surveillance of the population by Government agencies. The more recent Edward Snowden revelations of the NSA spying scandal, further underscores this alarming increase in the curtailment of liberties and freedom of expression.

Internationally, we have seen the entrenchment of authoritarian and repressive regimes around the globe, including China, North Korea, Iran, and Russia. Bashar al Assad's brutal

1

slaughter and gassing of the population in Syria's civil war is a horrendous example of how far fascist dictators will go to maintain power. Vladimir Putin's Russia increasingly resembles a return to the old Soviet Union days. Putin's land grabs in Georgia and Crimea not only threaten the Ukraine but all of Russia's neighbors and international stability as well. Furthermore, his domestic policies of media control and general repression of freedom of speech, the introduction of anti-homosexual laws, and "mistrust of the west propaganda" weakens the development of democracy and freedom for the Russian people.

It is therefore, imperative to establish a clear understanding of what fascism is, how it develops, and how it threatens all of us. This book is an attempt to do just that; to define fascism in all its forms and stages of development. There is an urgent need for the world to understand the evil shadow of fascism stalking us, and the need to prevent its perpetuation into the future. It is my sincere hope that this book will assist humanity in this endeavor by clarifying, in no uncertain terms, what we are up against, and how we can resist and eventually stamp out this insidious malignancy called fascism.

INTRODUCTION

When most people today hear the word 'fascism,' they think of a political system or party, which they immediately identify with Nazism and its modern offshoots. Fascism, they believe, exists elsewhere; not in a democratic society. Idealistically and dangerously myopic, they are oblivious to reality. For fascism is not a political system or party per se, but a specific "Weltanschauung;" a specific attitude towards, and a philosophy of the world, including life, people, love and work. Its source lies in the alienated individual raised and conditioned in an authoritarian societal structure, which includes rigid institutions, codes of morality, ideology, and thought. Indeed, projecting these criteria to the contemporary scene, whether we like to recognize it or not, fascism is alive and well in our own 'democratic' backyards.

Such public naiveté is largely due to the fact that we lack specific knowledge about the critical question of the sources of fascistic mentality. Even with the notorious example of the German brand of fascism, Nazism, accessible historical works tend to present the phenomenon as a 'fait accompli,' and instead dwell solely upon its heinous consequences. In such works the unspoken premise is that only the Germans, or possibly the Japanese, could somehow create and nourish such a monster.

Biases of this sort merely reflect the inescapable fact that human history has, for the most part, always been recorded through the partial eyes of the conquerors and victors of wars. Total and irrational vilification of 'the enemy,' however, is, as we shall see, in

3

itself a fascistic trait. Although vilification allows the victor to avoid any shred of guilt for any actions taken, it also unfortunately negates any objective attempt to comprehend the motivations of 'the enemy' from its own perspective. Their actions are seen as simply a 'necessary' result of their obvious 'wickedness'. The opportunity to learn from the totality of the experience is forfeited to convenience; an understanding of the rational development of fascistic mentality, and how it relates to the present world, is missed.

It is therefore, hardly coincidental that two of the few books which deal specifically with objective analyses of the sociological and psychological roots of fascism in general, were written by people who experienced the development of the phenomenon first-hand before being forced to flee it. Both books, however, appeared before the end of World War II. Wilhelm Reich's " Massen Psychologie des Faschismus" was published in 1933; Eric Fromm's " Escape from Freedom" in 1941. Without being able to take into consideration the totality of the Second World War and its aftermath, these analyses, while most valuable, are necessarily incomplete.

This book seeks to remedy this situation. Its purpose is three-fold: to produce an awareness of the intrinsic and universal nature of fascism, and the conditions which breed it; to explore the contemporary arena of fascism, and to take a look at where we are going from here.

I

FASCISM AND ITS SOURCES

F ascism is not a political party itself, although a political party can be fascistic. Rather, it is a particular 'Weltanschauung', a world view, a philosophy of life, or attitude towards the world in general. As such, it is not peculiar to only the 'villains' of World War II: the Germans, Italians and Japanese. It is an international phenomenon which permeates all organizations of human society in all nations. There is German, American, Italian, Japanese, Russian, Spanish, African, Chinese, Israeli and Arab fascism. Fascism exists in Europe, North and South America, Africa, Asia and the Middle East. Not restricted to any particular economic system, fascism can be found on both sides of the Iron Curtain, in both the Soviet and American economic empires. There can be fascistic democracy (McCarthy in America), fascistic socialism (Hitler in Nazi Germany), fascistic communism (Stalin in Russia), and a fascistic monarchy (Franco in Spain). A reflection of the mentality of the people, fascism permeates many political groups, including the 'left' as well as the 'right'.

Fascism is not merely a political ideology bestowed upon a hapless people. Its source is in the individual, and it is the collective energies of many individuals which produce the political manifestations we have learned to equate so singularly and

5

externally as fascism. Furthermore, all individuals in our society are fascistic; it is only the degree that varies. Its genesis lies in two separate yet interlocking motivations. On the one hand, is the alienated individual who when feeling helpless, ineffective and incapable of acting on his/her own, creates a demand for external guidance. On the other is the ruling interest group or individual who perceives that this need can be used for its own gain by providing the 'order'. As these two factions interact, each fostering its own interest, the system is self-reinforcing. Demand creates supply, and supply perpetuates demand and when the emotional climate nurtures the need for external control, all too often authoritarian institutions develop.

This distinction between the perpetrator and the subservient individual, however, is more theoretical than functional, for the two roles rarely exist as clearly separate in actual individuals. Most people learn to function in both roles to some degree, choosing whichever role is most beneficial in a given situation. Each individual is the victim as well as the villain of fascism. Because of this interlocking of roles, an analysis of the sociological/psychological development of fascism in the individual, cannot neatly separate the two. Hence the term 'authoritarian individual' will be used to denote the person conditioned to assume his/her role in the interlocking dynamics of fascism, that of both the perpetrator and the subservient individual.

The dynamics of authoritarian/fascistic social conditioning is such a subtle process that most individuals in our society are oblivious to its influences. Since the fascistic 'Weltanschauung' is, in essence, an attitude towards human behavior and human development, it can most clearly be understood through contrast with a non-authoritarian model of human growth and development.

The non-authoritarian recognizes that each and every human, under favorable social conditions, is an honest, dependable, cooperative and industrious individual, capable of love and rational thinking. Each person is thus respected and supported in his/her personal growth and development. Natural impulses are not repressed, but allowed to expend their energy, and are dealt with on a personal level. Central to the non-authoritarian 'Weltanschauung' is the premise that human beings have the innate ability to face problems, take the responsibility for their own growth and development, find their own uniqueness, as well as confront and cope with weaknesses or failures.

In contrast, the premise of the authoritarian individual is that traits such as honesty, cooperation and industriousness must be imposed upon the individual, and that individuals must earn respect. Natural, or animalistic impulses are seen as unfortunate phenomena which must be blocked/repressed, for their expenditure is innately uncontrollable and unproductive once released, and therefore, a dire threat requiring constant vigilance. As the antithesis to the concept of active personal relatedness, the authoritarian individual vaguely perceives happiness and fulfillment as external, universal and as pre-defined goals which are not self-definable, and thus not directly achievable through independent action, learning and growth. Instead, this externalized, vicarious conception of personal happiness and fulfillment, is felt to be best achieved through resigning oneself to acquiescence and compliance with, even surrender and submission to, 'the powers that be'.

Although few of us would openly ascribe to the latter ideology, few of us can honestly say we perfectly personify the non-authoritarian perspective either. The great majority of Americans, and humans in general, fluctuate somewhere between these two extremes. It is this relative level of fascism which defines each individual's world view, and collectively, that of the political mood of the country.

The disclaimer of the non-authoritarian view of human nature, however, is the phrase "under favorable social conditions", for despite the individual's innate striving for growth, society can serve to thwart, if not completely frustrate this natural impulse. Using this perspective, we can begin to explore the societal conditioning which serves to reinforce the authoritarian 'Weltanschauung' over the non-authoritarian.

At the core are a multitude of societal restrictions imposed upon each member, which serve to crush any strivings for active personal relatedness. Yet, in broad psychological terms, it is this very inner striving to grow, love and learn, that makes our lives and our environment relative and meaningful. When this is not happening, as in much of the modern world where life has lost its human proportions, there can be little real sense of this personal growth towards an expanded consciousness. Rather, the capacities of the self are felt to be ineffective. Individual powerlessness and inhibited spontaneity create people with a disintegrated sense of reality, making them feel afraid and doubtful. Unable to relate, people find their own individuality to be a burden and feel isolated. They seek a way out of the need to establish genuine relatedness, and this is the foundation of the authoritarian personality. These individuals want to give up the task of creating identities, and instead unconsciously long to submerge themselves in a sense of powerfulness greater than each feels alone.

In equally broad physiological terms, when human natural impulses are blocked or thwarted, repressed rather than expended, they do not simply disappear. Science now perceives the human body as an incredibly complex and delicate circuit of electro-chemical charges, similar to the ancient Eastern concept of human auras and energy flows through interior pathways with focalized centers called chakras. Energy blockages caused by inhibitions and unresolved tension cause these bodily circuits to slow down and freeze, manifesting in muscle tension or other physiological disorders. Such conditions prevent the individual from radiating the totality of his/her own power, uniqueness and purposefulness.

Self-alienation due to inability to deal with feelings and desires, creates 'frozen energy states' in minds and bodies. This rigidity in the body is referred to as 'character armor' or 'muscular armor'. Such disorders reduce the bodily energy flow and restricts it from flowing freely throughout the body. When these blockages are softened or broken down, movement and emotions appear; one feels energized, full of life, and experiences a new and heightened sense of 'being'. Many therapies and healing disciplines have all been developed to help people release these blockages and clear the energy flow, at least temporarily. Important in this process is learning to take the responsibility for oneself; the realization that these blockages are the results of one's own thoughts, actions or inactions.

The more exact nature of the many socially imposed restrictions upon the individual will consume the rest of this chapter. Let it be stated at the outset, however, that the oldest and most effective form of imposing human restrictions is guilt. It is one of the most pervasively effective means of control over others. Guilt is innately linked with pleasure/morality, and of all that is pleasurable in the human experience, sexuality has been the most focalized target of fascist conditioning, and the strongest weapon in the arsenal of morality. Sexuality makes such a good target precisely because it is common to all people, and is perhaps the strongest instinct other than survival itself. Analyses of the psychological processes which govern psychic life have shown that sexuality, is a primary motor of psychic life.[1]

If sufficient restrictions are externally imposed upon a group of people, their psychic energy can be channeled and used by those in control of the restrictions. Integral to the mass psychology of fascistic conditioning are the indispensable accessories to mind control; the preoccupation with such ideological tactics as the idealization of order and regimentation, ritualizing the giving and obeying of orders, blind submission to authority, strict adherence to predefined concepts of 'good' and 'bad', and conformity to rigid codes of morality. Included in the latter, is the repression of spontaneous sexuality and all other forms of natural pleasure which are of a free, unattached and unregulated nature. Reinforcing this system is the promotion of fear and paranoia, rooted in deep-seated feelings of guilt, self-negation and alienation, all of which are inseparably connected with today's dominant patriarchal order.

Embodying any societal order, and vital to its dynamics are the component political, spiritual and familial orders, represented by the state, church and family. Each of these structures reflects as well as influences the prevalent degree of fascism in any given society. Of these, the family has the earliest and perhaps greatest influence. It is the family which first molds the individuals who must then function within the larger society.

THE PATRIARCHAL FAMILY

In any analysis of the traditional American family structure, an understanding of the term patriarchal is most imperative. The word patriarchal like fascism itself, is often used yet seldom fully understood. In both cases, our historical experiences with the terms have served to change their original focus and obscure their meaning.

Patriarchy, like fascism, is a 'Weltanschauung', a world view towards life in general and human nature in specific. Patriarchy has no inherent connection to the male gender, just as matriarchy has no inherent connection to the female gender. There is, however, a relationship between the traditional societal conception of the male role and patriarchy, as well as the female role, and matriarchy. This relationship has developed from ages of historical association, rather than from any innate connection. Long before the rise of patriarchy, matriarchy was the norm in the ancient world, including in early Egypt and Europe.

Ignoring for the moment the gender/role camouflage, we can see how the patriarchal 'Weltanschauung' directly relates to fascism by tracing its origin to the authoritarian model of human development previously discussed. In contrast, the concept of matriarchy can be traced to the non-authoritarian conception of human nature. In the context of a familial structure, the matriarchal/non-authoritarian family is organized for the purpose of supporting the personal growth and development of all its members, particularly the children. Aside from material existence needs, this goal is primarily accomplished through encouragement

10

to explore, find and perfect their own unique potential. Central to this process is the premise that all individuals innately possess the necessary motivation, and tools to find their own most productive and rewarding role in the collective unit of the family. Personal growth is seen as primarily a singular process for which each individual can and must take one's own responsibility for failure, as well as success.

As a result, love, cooperation, mutual trust and respect, as well as the encouragement of self-analysis, critical thinking and independent action are the primary necessities, and the matriarchal family structure evolved to best meet these needs. Thus, there is no need for a hierarchy or class structure, for no member is considered more or less expendable than any other. Decisions are collective, for each member's perspective is respected and encouraged for the well being of the whole, as well as the individual. Strict and predefined functional roles and the resulting status and privilege have no place in the matriarchal scheme of family.

Each member must find his/her own function based upon the constant interplay between collective needs and personal interest, ability and growth. Since each function is considered equally important to the welfare of the greater whole, individual roles are relatively flexible, varying upon this constantly changing interrelationship between collective and individual needs.

In the matriarchal family, parents love the children no matter what they may do; they believe that eventually they can and will 'get it together', for they trust the basic nature of the self in every human being. Furthermore, since the basic responsibility for 'success' remains with the child, the parents are free from the burden of guilt, and can therefore more objectively reflect alternatives to the child. In the end, as long as the child takes the responsibility for his/her own actions, simplified by the fact that the parents refuse the burden, then the child must act upon conscience and learn from the experience.

In the patriarchal family this is not the case. The children must prove themselves worthy by being obedient, submissive and 'good' in the authoritarian sense of the word first, and then the parental figure will extend love and respect towards them. This contrast is explained by the fact that the premise of the patriarchal family, and thus, the resulting family structure, is strikingly opposed to that of the matriarchal.

Rather than being individually defined, the patriarchal family member's growth and development is primarily seen within the narrower context of collective efficiency towards a singular material definition of successful personal growth. The term individual becomes equated with 'production unit' and personal growth and development takes on the connotation of 'marketable skills', as truly individual strivings progressively become more and more subordinated to the inflated sense of material 'need'.

It is therefore, easier to understand the concurrent development of the authoritarian attitude that such human qualities as honesty, cooperation, loyalty, respect and industriousness must be imposed upon the individual, for the patriarchal perspective of each of these quality's definition is vastly different from that of the matriarchal perspective. If patriarchal family members were to be encouraged to aspire to their own definition of personal happiness and success, many would choose a path in which single-minded material success would not be that important, and thus would not be seen as being (materially) industrious. If, however, this single focus upon material success can be effectively instilled upon each member of the group, then the family unit will gain tremendous productive advantage and economic power over others. This example, at the microcosm/familial level, of the patriarchal goal of economic power over other families, is the same dynamic discernible at the macrocosm/societal level, where the economic power of the patriarchal state dominates other states, or the economic power of the patriarchal church dominates other churches.

Since the family order of Western civilization, as well as the resulting societal orders of church and state, have for centuries been rooted in the patriarchal 'Weltanschauung', any analysis of contemporary fascism must begin by taking a critical look at the authoritarian conditioning within the family in particular. In such a study, however, it must be clear that the traditional association of the male role with patriarchy and the female role with matriarchy is deceptive. In matriarchy, males and females were equal. Females did not intrinsically have a greater role under matriarchy, for it is essentially roll -less. Rather, the patriarchy is so identified with the traditional male role that matriarchy is female identified by default. It is also important to realize that when a society is so pervasively patriarchal as ours, both men and women are similarly conditioned by it. Although the traditional role of women allows them to carry some of the matriarchal attitudes into our patriarchal society, it is usually only those that the patriarchy deems 'appropriate', and relatively little value is placed upon them. Because of this pervasive societal conditioning, women can be, and often are, just as patriarchal in character as men. This is particularly true when women strive for, or find themselves in, positions of power over others, for the patriarchy is seemingly the only role model, even though it is the traditionally identified 'masculine' role that is being emulated.

It should now be easier to see how it is the patriarchal family that is the factory producing the structure and ideology of societal fascism. As the result of the authoritarian decision to emphasize collective over individual development, material growth over mental, emotional or spiritual development, the role, structure and dynamics of the family, and thus, society as well, changed. Tactics which effectively enforce rather than support dominate. Instead of the independence of each family member, their collective dependence now becomes the goal. These goals are primarily accomplished through the development of centralized control within the family, resulting in a family hierarchy. As we shall later explore, this same development on the societal level produces a class hierarchy, and centralized roles of control in church and state as well.

The authoritarian state has its representative in every patriarchal family, symbolized by the role of the father, and as such, he is the authoritarian state's most valuable tool. Within the family, a strictly proscribed regime exists, based upon role and age status, rather than a free exchange of equally valued functional duties. Ready-made roles, modes of 'individual' behavior, and clichés replace spontaneous and truly individualistic interaction.

Since the central role of the family, aside from that of an economic unit, is the socialization of the children, the manner in which this task is handled profoundly effects their natures. Unfortunately, the patriarchal family is characterized by the fearful subservience on the part of the children to the demands of the parents, which results in an early suppression of all impulses not acceptable to the parents. As previously noted, if sufficient restrictions are externally imposed upon a group of people, their psychic energy can be perceived by them as an uncontrollable burden. This 'burden' can then quite easily be channeled and redirected for the advantage of those who control the restrictions.

The first and most pervasive parental demand which the child encounters, and perhaps the one most central to the blocking of the child's further strivings towards active personal relatedness and growth, is the repression of infantile sexuality, and the resultant implantation of guilt. Strict punishment of masturbation, self-curiosity, nudity, homosexuality, bodily functions, un-gender-like behavior, and even 'dirty' or 'sinful' thoughts is the standard practice of the patriarchal parent.

Such impulses in the child, however, are not deprived of their strength. On the contrary, their repression serves to intensify the need for sexual release, in the extreme manifesting as various psychic disturbances. It is also critical to realize that this sexual guilt, from the perspective of the child, effectively removes his/her own sexuality from conscious control. Here is hatched the first inkling of the authoritarian premise that animalistic instincts must be controlled, and hence the need for external controls to enforce upon the individual, a development that is innately not self-regulatory.

This original conflict between a child's desires and parental prohibitions lives on within the adult. Wilhelm Reich's analysis is very emphatic in its assertion that the sexual inhibitions of the child block his or her way to rational thinking and emotional balance, due to the resulting internal conflict between instinct and 'morals'.[2] This externally imposed sense of a universal morality, often unconscious in the adult, acts against the individual's recognition of his/her own sexual needs, blocking a considerable portion of the individual's psychic energy. Sexual repression explains the resistance of our society to even recognize, much less deal with, infantile and adolescent sexual needs, as well as a good measure of the resulting adolescent rebelliousness that is so typical of patriarchal society.

Psychologist Else Frenkel-Brunswick, in a study on the development of the authoritarian personality, states that "the lack of an internalized and individualized approach to the child on the part of the parents, as well as a tendency to transmute mainly a set of conventional rules and customs, may be considered as interfering with the development of a clear-cut personal identity in the growing child.'[3] This failure of children raised in the authoritarian family to develop a clear-cut personal identity, makes it difficult for them not only to have a strong sense of their unique selfness, but also to genuinely relate with other people.

Psychologist William R. Morrow, in a study of 'anti-democratic behavior', states that this failure to personalize human interaction and relationship is the basic cause of receptivity to authoritarian ideology.[4] The fascist individual, upon meeting a stranger, will eye that person suspiciously, and more easily see him/her as a potential threat than be open to a possible positive exchange. The non-fascist person, in comparison, would be open and receptive to a stranger, anticipating the potential of an interesting and exciting exchange.

Due to the suppression of much of one's own feelings and impulses, this externally imposed 'moral' conflict also creates a need for release through projection upon external scapegoats. Moral indignation first experienced in the attitude of one's parents towards oneself results in the repression of instinctual impulses, and a redirection of this frustration towards others. The tremendous anxiety caused by the fear of straying from the predefined roles and rules transmitted by the parent, an essentially self-negating submission to authority, creates conscious or unconscious resentment and feelings of victimization, which are conveniently displaced through hostility towards scapegoats permitted by the parents. In learning respect for power and authority, the children simultaneously learn to release feelings of personal ineffectiveness and powerlessness safely upon an even weaker group. The love of power and hatred of weakness syndrome so typical of authoritarian individuals, can thus be seen, as an outgrowth from parental attitudes towards the individual as a child.

In hating the weak and loving the strong, however, they are not consciously realizing that they are also among the weak, and as such are being irrational and self-destructive. Nonetheless, by discovering some segment of society even more suppressed than they are, they can gain a temporary and relative sense of power and prestige, along with feelings of honor, morality and 'normalcy'.

There are, of course, vested interests within a society which are well aware of the need for an outlet for people's frustrations, and they also know which groups are potentially profitable to be discriminated against. Discrimination serves an important role for those in power, for they can in fact turn any group they wish into the scapegoat, and it is thus not uncommon for fascist leaders to instill and implant ideas of discrimination in an authoritarian-dominated society for very specific purposes. It is not accidental that by discriminating against the Jews in Nazi Germany, the National Socialists gained vast wealth and material power lost by Jewish people. African American and Spanish-speaking Americans were/are not only a scapegoat, but also a critically important source of cheap labor in the economic structure, for which an elaborate rationalization for their sub-human treatment had to be contrived. Lesbians and Gay Men are not only a most convenient outlet for very thinly veiled sexual hostilities, but are also a direct threat to the existing 'normalcy' of restrictive sex roles, compulsive marriage and sexual denial/guilt which are essential to retaining power over the masses.

Ironically, most scapegoating is laced with the 'moralism' that authoritarian individuals are actually attempting to rebel against on a subconscious level, however ineffectively. This hostility particularly appears as open hate and contempt towards those who can be objectified by their anti-sexual righteousness; towards the 'immoral' people whose natural sexuality and unrestricted lifestyles potently ignite the authoritarian's fears of 'moral decline', visions of a conveniently twisted 'Sodom and Gomorrah'* and a return to 'barbarism, lasciviousness and sexual filth'.

*Biblical condemnation of homosexuality in the story of Sodom and Gomorrah hinges solely upon a sexual interpretation of the word 'know' in the crowd's command to Lot "bring them out so that we may know them". Since linguists maintain that there was no such ancient connotation of the word, today's enlightened Biblical scholars interpret the 'sin' of Sodom and Gomorrah as being inhospitality.

To seek compensation through projection into the outside world against such people as prostitutes, divorcees, homosexuals or unwed mothers, can be seen as merely an attempt to ascribe one's own feared and repressed qualities, however unconsciously, to the external world. Stereotyping and scapegoating become all-encompassing solutions, a handy formula for dealing with situations unconsciously laden with one's own fear and pain. Stereotyping becomes 'stereopathy' as all is seen in terms of predefined 'good and bad', 'them and us', emphasizing all the evil 'them out there' who can be blamed for anything and everything. Personal shortcomings can thus be avoided and covered over, with conformity the major expression of this lack of internal honesty. In fact, the litmus test for establishing the degree of fascism within a society can be determined by observing the way in which women, homosexuals, ethnic or religious minorities, as well as the mentally and physically challenged, are treated. The more poorly they are treated, the higher the degree of fascism.

Besides this family conditioned susceptibility to a conventional 'morality' and set of values, Frankel-Brunswick found that this same submission to authority, and lack of independent and critical judgment, leads the individual to be gullible to unsound and destructive social influences as well, such as political propaganda and religious dogma.[5] Thus is created the potential for not only masses of people to be kept alienated, fearful, restricted, inexperienced, separated from each other and powerless, but also dangerously dependent upon super-leaders and their supra-individual 'laws'.

Returning once again to the microcosm level of the patriarchal family, the lack of an individualized approach to the child, and the transmittal of only a conventional set of moral 'rules', simultaneously results in the failure of the child to be encouraged to develop any truly personal defined sense of morality and/or self-control. The development of ethical values based upon the child's own experiences, observation and human interaction are likely to be sacrificed by the child to the expediency and parental reward of stock answers. Unfortunately, such programmed responses will be much less relevant to the infinite variety of real life situations the child will later encounter, or perhaps choose not to encounter. Instead, what little personal discernment that is developed, is almost completely limited to fear of external punishment, social failure and ostracism.[6]

This fear of being left alone upon one's own devices is perhaps one of the greatest anxieties of authoritarian individuals. Independence of a spontaneous sort is an alien concept, for not only is there no sense of self-regulation, but no sense of even how one could regulate the self. They are afraid of their own sexual needs, for example, because they never learned to even acknowledge them, much less handle them. They have a low sense of confidence in themselves. Rather than take upon themselves the task of striving for personal growth and development, they usually decline the responsibility for their decisions and action and instead demand external guidance. In case of failure, at least 'they' can be blamed for it.

It should now be easier to perceive why and how the patriarchal factory produces children who tend towards being inhibited, timid, apprehensive, shy, obedient and respectful, yet powerful in their strong dedication to the defense of conformity; 'good' and 'well-adjusted' in the authoritarian sense of the words. The rebellious forces have been paralyzed, for the mere thought of rebellion is laden with anxiety. Rebellion would, in effect, invalidate all the years of submission to external authority that were the source of the alienation to begin with, and furthermore, there is little sense of what could possibly replace external authority. Beginning with the sexual inhibition of the infant, each step towards 'successful' submission is accompanied by equal inhibition of independent thinking, rationality and the critical faculties, producing an individual who is adjusted to the authoritarian order and obedient to whoever sets and controls the order. Unfortunately, most traditional psychology has long referred to this process as "positive adjustment to society".

The more helpless the individual feels in his/her upbringing, the more strongly s/he identifies with external authority, creating an illusionary sense of 'oneness' with it, as compensation. This conditioning of respect and fear is later easily transferred to other authoritarian images such as the church or state, the guru or the Fuehrer. Through the creation of this psychological attachment to the external power, however, the individual gives up the potential to realize a truly individual and unique identity. For example, when the child leaves the close-knit and over-protective patriarchal family, s/he must cope with the reality of being alone, of being an entity relatively separate from others for the first time. Facing the world, in all its overpowering aspects, alone and unprepared, often seems threatening and dangerous. Feelings of powerlessness and anxiety arise, often followed by impulses to give up one's individuality and overcome the seemingly precarious situation by attempting to submerge oneself in something, even anything, that offers security. Unprepared to go out and explore, to really experience their freedom, such an individual will tend to throw away an excellent opportunity for personal growth by either returning home or jumping headlong into another well defined and structured situation, one where personal conduct has conveniently been previously ordered and defined by someone who 'knows better'.

As we have seen, the patriarchal family creates and nurtures the initial formation of the authoritarian personality. The example of sexual repression is only one of the many natural human impulses that we, through conditioning, learn to suppress and frustrate. Eventually, we can suppress such a wide variety of our natural impulses that we become alienated from our very selves. Related to sexual repression, and consistent with the patriarchal tactic of the use of fear to suppress and force submission, is the pervasive family conditioning upon the basis of gender roles. The strictest of roles according to sexual gender, patented upon the super-human images of the father and the mother, are basic to the patriarchal structure of order and control.

Although such roles serve to strengthen the family as an economic unit through extreme specialization within the prescribed function of the role, each member is personally weakened through the inescapable result of total dependency upon the roles of the others. Each role tends to become so extreme that it soon becomes ineffectual without the 'balance' of the other, 'opposite' role. Thus, the authoritarian notion of the achievement of a complete personal identity through external union can be better understood, for the concept of personal completeness becomes a goal that lies outside of the self, rather than being seen as an internal process. Compulsive marriage is understandably not only the rule, but seemingly the only alternative as well, for individuals thus conditioned.

Through the most persuasive of conditioning, the child's acceptance of the prescribed role behavior is usually achieved at a very early age in the patriarchal family. Although this acceptance can be seen as 'easier' for the child, the submission to such a limited view of one's potential growth and development is debilitating. As Frenkel-Brunswick notes in her psychological studies, the authoritarian's repression of much of his/her natural, spontaneous impulses affects not only the ability to enjoy sexuality and sensuality, but also such passive pleasures as affection, companionship and the sense of well-being other than material well-being. Instead, much of this is replaced by a flight into mobility, constant activity, external proofs of 'normalcy', and the striving for an externally imposed definition of 'success', particularly through material striving.[7] This is especially true of the male role in the patriarchal scheme of things.

The male role is 'success' oriented, compulsive and competitive, with little room for passivity or softness because of the strong taboos against such 'unmanly' attributes. To escape the resulting fear of sensitivity and openness, males most often try to bolster themselves through pseudo-toughness and anti-sensitive defenses. The strong need in the patriarchal male to conceive of himself as an ideal of super-human 'masculinity' is a hallmark of early conditioning in the family. The subconsciously weak sense of ego-self results in conscious protections of over-aggressiveness and intimidation, for to look at one's own shortcomings, or to be forced to, would be fatal to that image. Instead, he is compulsive in his need for external verification that he is standard, not weak or 'queer', and therefore all right.

Another compensation is found in the admiration of, and the search for power. According to Frenkel-Brunswick, an inability to create affectionate and individualized interpersonal relationships, along with the conception of a dangerous and threatening world filled with imaginary foes, are often found to be underlying factors causing the authoritarian lust for power.[8] In this quest for power, there is a strong tendency to utilize everything and everyone as a means to an end. Ruthless opportunism is seen as an essential attribute of masculine success, including the exploitation of women. Sex, to the patriarchal male, is often a conquest seen in terms of status and power.[9]

Indeed, psychologist Morrow points out that many authoritarian men seem basically rejected, and to have almost given up the hope of ever experiencing genuine love: "They speak as if they dislike and fear themselves as well as others. Their main energies seem to be devoted to defending themselves against any sense of weakness, chiefly striving for external status, power and 'proofs' of masculinity. The result is a power-oriented character structure driven to attack out-groups as symbols of their own suppressed characteristics."[10] Morrow also found that fascistic individuals reveal a decidedly heterosexual orientation which is externalized, contemptuous and exploitative. In many instances this is characterized by a "flight into heterosexual activity" which is accompanied by obsessive fear of homosexuality, or homophobia.[11]

In contrast, the equally super-human role of the mother in the patriarchal schemata must include all those qualities missing from the role of the father, and thus externally balance the role of power and strength which characterizes the masculine. Unless called upon by circumstance to perform the other role, a task she is usually totally unconditioned for, the patriarchal mother image is one of passivity and subservience to men. The mother has no needs of her own, and instead serves as the emotional filling station for the more aggressively out-going males. She is restricted to 'Kinder, Kueche und Kirche' – (Children, Kitchen and Church), a role to be performed backstage, out of the public eye, and thus the self direction of her personal power, is thwarted and indirectly used by the dominant males.

Sayings such as "behind every great man is a great woman" reflect the patriarchal role of woman/mother/wife, who is allowed so little active self- effectiveness that her natural striving for any self-verification is most conveniently directed vicariously through her husband and children. Thus, the goal of becoming a Doctor's wife,(or a Doctor's mother/mother-in-law) is a logical outcome of an imposed need for external self-realization. As the Doctor's wife, she can latch onto his recognition, status and power, and at least gain the illusion of the personal power which she herself has been denied.

Although the patriarchal order exerts its toll in sexual inhibition upon each member of the family unit, the male role carries the most sexual liberty, while that of the female is perhaps the most irrationally restrictive. Most tragically, the damaging burden of patriarchal inhibition is dramatically demonstrated by recent studies which show that not only have a large portion of American women/mothers never experienced an orgasm, but many are not aware that they have not experienced one, for they are not aware that they are supposed to. In the patriarchal process of sexual denial and guilt, natural sexuality came to be looked down upon, distorted and debased to the point that any sexuality became something 'unnatural and filthy'. What is often overlooked, however, and as Reich notes, is the fact that this 'unnatural sexuality' is indeed not natural sexuality, but only the specific sexuality of the patriarchy.[12]

The shift of power from communal matriarchy to authoritarian patriarchy, was gradually achieved through the hierarchical system of order and control. In this shift, the economic interests of marriage, dowries and inheritance became major modes of exchange between people, exemplified by women being literally sold to men for keeps. Powerful males came to own women and children under the rule of permanent marriage, the central institution of patriarchy. It is still common to this day in our society for women and children who are physically brutalized by their husbands/ fathers, to be denied legal protection. In the statutes of much of our still archaic 'law', women and children are the property of the fathers, who are free to feel that occasionally 'their' wards need to be 'tamed'. Although women are finally gaining a modicum of legal protection, the continued status of children as property with virtually no legal rights of their own is rarely addressed.

The role of woman/mother, then, with its super-human burden of 'femininity', naturally produces intense feelings of victimization. This alienation is often 'safely' released through the stereotypical attribute of 'bitchiness', an understandable yet ineffectual direction of the feelings of powerlessness. It is an escape in that it is a projection of the entire difficulty upon others, relieving the self of the personal responsibility to actively change the situation. Exaggerated demands upon the husband as the provider is an example. The most destructive result of this alienation, however, occurs when the conditioning intrinsic to the female role produces only self-persecution and self-negation: the 'mea culpa syndrome' of Christianity, "through my fault, through my fault, through my most grievous fault."

Nonetheless, the female role is not without its supposed advantages, or else it could not have endured for so long. The sacrifice of personal power in order to gain a sense of security can be tempting, and in fact, it is sold as the main 'privilege' of the female role. No matter how extensively we have been conditioned to equate the role model of masculine power with the only sense of power, and that therefore feminine power is weak, we should not be taken in by this duality, for on a larger perspective each role is weak. As we have seen, true personal power lies in the internal synthesis of the beneficial attributes of each role. The supposed power of the male role is destructive to the self and to others regardless of the gender which strives to use it, for males are equally enslaved in their role as providers and defenders. Authoritarian raised males are not only fodder for the work force and the military, but their lives are expendable at times of economic imperialism and war, which patriarchal societies thrive on. Men in our society suffer at the other end of the pole from women, children and the elderly.

As a role model, men are not supposed to be sensitive, feeling, emotional or warm. Instead, in a patriarchal society they are expected to be cold, calculating, defensive, rigid, strong and responsible. As a result, men often feel alienated from a major portion of their nature. Having lost contact with their sensitive half, their subconscious, they are actually emotionally crippled. Not only have men given up their emotional power by relying externally upon women as their emotional filling stations, they have also taken on the responsibility to protect and provide for the entire family unit, a tremendously restrictive burden which saps them of energy for any other type of personal growth. This, in turn, further weakens the position of women, children and the elderly, who are somehow not expected to be capable of being responsible for their own needs. Men in the patriarchy tend to be seriously guilt ridden by responsibility, as well as emotionally impaired, symbolized by constant work in an alienating factory or office and a patriotic death for the family, God and flag. More often, however, the end comes through a much less romanticized heart attack many years before the demise of the wife.

The power accredited to the authoritarian male is two-sided and schizophrenic. He is taught to be aggressive, commanding and authoritative, yet at the same time he must be obedient and submissive to all authorities higher than himself, all the while being unemotional and seemingly in control. To even let on that he is victimized would be a sign of weakness, a serious flaw to his masculine image.

Although this schizophrenic situation is also evident in the female role, it would seem that it is the actual emotional weakness of the male role, which blocks the acknowledgement that a problem even exists. Since women can more easily risk appearing 'weak', they are more often able to acknowledge the problems inherent in their limited role, the first step in the process of actively doing something about it. It seems understandable that women, through the support of the women's liberation movement, should be the first to find the emotional strength to begin the laborious process of challenging and redefining their roles. If, however, the goal is actually human liberation, then there must inevitably follow a men's liberation movement in which males also find the emotional strength to acknowledge and confront their own oppression. Women have led the way by demonstrating the healing power of sisterhood, and the task for men is to overcome their conditioning to see all other men as only threats and potential competitors. When men can truly open up to other men as potential brothers, then they are on their way to seeing women as potential sisters.

THE ECONOMICS OF PATRIARCHY

In discussing the authoritarian personality, it is necessary to devote attention to the economic aspects involved in the development of the patriarchy. Since social economics is such a critical factor in the quality of each individual's material existence, it greatly effects the development of their general 'Weltanschauung' as well.

The present patriarchal order and the fall of matriarchy, resulted from fundamental structural and ideological changes within the family and the larger tribal grouping of families. This process was typified by the economic separatism of male dominated authoritarian families, which had succeeded in gaining power through competitive control of material production. This new emphasis upon competitive materialism, was what could be considered the first form of capitalism, and was accompanied by male domination over women, children and the elderly through role status within the family and tribal groupings.

As the most competitively successful tribes gained power over others through their economic advantage, particularly their resulting ability to support a military class, city-states, nations and even vast empires arose. This process took many centuries, and is, in fact, what the great majority of our present body of history records. Seen chiefly through the eyes of the lineage of the victors, it depicts our sense of human progress, genius, intrigue and glory, as well as human savagery, misery and folly. If all of human history can be summarized in any manner, perhaps the only thing that can be said is that we owe practically all of what we have inherited today in this 'ascent of man' to patriarchy.

Central to the question at hand, however, is that concurrent with this ascent, there also developed divisions within the larger society based upon similar value judgments of societal roles, status and power as prescribed within the patriarchal family. Although differences had always existed between people in terms of interests, skills and abilities, and thus loose classes in the sense that cabinet making is different from chopping wood, never before the advent of the patriarchy had there been sharp value judgments put on these differences. Now, classes came into existence which claimed to be of more collective value, in that they could exert a greater amount of economic control over others. Perhaps their greatest persuasion was that they could force others into believing it. This sense of hierarchy so intrinsic to patriarchy, eventually resulted in the rise of ruling classes of economic, intellectual and spiritual power. This authoritarian perspective to human value and worth, can be illustrated by the medieval theologians who seriously debated whether or not women could possess souls, as well as the much later question of whether or not African Americans were human.

Beginning with tribal land claims based upon usage rights, the first economic power was based upon control of land, culminating in our present concept of personal property. This, however, has not always been the case, the Native Americans being good examples. Their conception of the earth was that it belonged to everyone and no one; to each and every creature which walked upon it, swam below it, or flew above it. Unfortunately, many could not apply these principles to a greater whole than the tribe, and inter-tribal warfare punctuated this idealized reality even before the disastrous appearance of the white man.

Once the patriarchal concept of individual ownership of the land had succeeded, social stratification was primarily based upon the differentiation between those who owned the land and/or could defend it, and those who were landless and could only sell their physical labor for the privilege of using other's land. At some point in each society, however, there developed a definable class of people whose skill in crafts/professions gave them unique economic assets and status, placing them between the landed and the landless. Simplifying immensely for our limited present need, as well as using value-charged words, we can consider those who own the land and/or the means of production as the 'upper', or 'ruling class'; those whose primary economic asset is their unique acquired marketable skill as the 'middle class'; and those whose 'only' asset is their physical labor as the 'lower', or 'working class'.

A closer analysis of this middle class is most relevant, for modern mass fascism coincides with the entrance of the middle class into society as a major social force. Nazism in Germany, for example, was originally a middle class movement of particular appeal to the lower middle class, or what is presently referred to as 'middle America'. As a result of its unique authoritarian character structure, the middle class is an enormous social power which far outweighs its economic power. It is also the repression of this class, as we shall see, that is to a large extent responsible for keeping patriarchy alive so long, despite its blatant contradictions.

The middle class, then, is by nature always looking upward, trying to differentiate itself from the lower class and trying to identify with the much coveted upper class. Studies have repeatedly shown that many more Americans have a conception of themselves as 'upper middle class' than their economic condition, education, or level of skill would actually indicate in a true sociological sense. The core ideology of this middle class is based upon the principles of thrift, hard work and competition, for it is these traits, along with a little luck, that got them to where they are. The upper class supports these principles of thrift, hard work and competition, for it is directly to their advantage, yet, they do not save, work or compete in the same sense at all. They own and control the land, the means of production and the banks, and thus profit from the thrift and hard work of the middle and lower class. To the upper class, competition, in its modern context, means monopolistic capitalism, syndicates, multi-national corporations and interlocking directorates. In the face of such 'competition', the middle class small entrepreneur inevitably fails.

Thus, the middle class develops a contradiction between their actual economic position and their thrifty, hard working and competitive ideology of aspiration. It may have gotten them to an insecure identity as middle class, but, contrary to the Hollywood myth, without a lot more that just thrift, hard work or competition alone, they will never attain upper class status. As well as desperately trying to keep up appearance, or the American 'keeping up with the Joneses', the middle class latches onto what they perceive are the upper class's attitudes and ideas in order to distinguish themselves from the lower class, with the accent on lower. However, as a result of such equalizing social forces as minimum wage laws and labor unions, the lower class blue collar worker often makes a comparable or even higher wage than the middle class white collar worker or small business operator. In their passion to distinguish themselves from the 'mere laborers', the middle class often finds that the only way in which this can be done is upon the much more intangible terms of their 'superior' attitudes. Stemming from the middle class's strict patriarchal conditioning, the 'moral' ideology of family, church and state have to make up for what is glaringly lacking in terms of economic prestige.

Frankel-Brunswick found that the more urgent the social status anxiety of the parents, the more they tend to adopt a rigid set of conventional values, viewing the child's behavior in these terms instead of the child's own needs.[13] These moralistic attitudes express themselves in ideas as well as behavior, in ideas of honor, pride, duty, sexual morality, patriotism, thrift, righteousness and cultural tastes, all of which mainly serve the purpose of snobbish distinction from the lower class. These same ideas constantly recur in the ideologies of fascism, particularly a mystical sense of honor: the necessity for self-control, sexual control and social control; family honor, personal honor, race honor and national honor. This identification with the need to fight temptation, fight against one's animalistic nature, and to uphold morality in general, develop into compulsive and highly emotionally charged ideas of superiority. Such ideas, however, are actually based upon feelings of inferiority, fear, guilt and personal ineffectiveness. In addition, the competitive nature of authoritarian society merely feeds into the fear and paranoia already at large.

As a result, the authoritarian middle class individual usually tries to establish a secure environment, an orderly and structured family, church and state. In doing so, the individual can feel a sense of security in his or her external environment to balance the internal insecurity. This projection towards external order is a form of fascist mysticism; believing the answer to one's uniqueness to be outside of oneself, beyond the reality of creating an inner security based upon personal experience.

This tendency to grasp at external supports is increased when a society goes through a social and economic collapse, as we shall see in the case of post World War I Germany. When the social and economic order give way, many portions of the population, especially the groups conscious of their former oppression, take the opportunity to develop new and alternative structures to replace those that have fallen. This upsurge of innovative radical energy develops innumerable ideas of personal, as well as, collective freedom and equality, which break down the old morals, attitudes and modes of behavior. After the initial rejoicing on the part of those that have liberated themselves, however, there almost inevitably follows a conservative reactionary movement fueled by those who see other's liberation as too threatening to their own traditionally ordered lifestyles. Out of this fear, they attempt to restore order by bringing back 'the good old days' of law and order. It is at this point that the danger of institutionalized and politicized fascism becomes possible.

As a group, the middle class is hardest hit by the collapse of the old moral and economic structures, leaving them feeling lost, frustrated, alienated and looking for an authoritative 'answer'.

Much of their material assets such as their income, paper money and bank savings are suddenly wiped out. In addition to the material loss, which we must remember is their primary reference for the definition of personal happiness and success, the breakdown of the moral structure serves to only increase their insecurity. All of this is not particularly new for the lower class. They will most definitely encounter increased hardship, but in terms of material assets, they have little to lose, and they never were that attached to the 'moral order' of the patriarchy anyway. It is their very economic situation that allows them to more successfully 'cope', for they have had plenty experience at it.

Unlike the upper class, which owns the factories, banks, international corporations and the land, none of which seriously lose their value in the long run if they play it right, the middle class, with its veneration of the ethic of thriftiness and hard work, sees the result of all this hard work devalued to worthlessness. Because of its authoritarian character structure, the middle class can usually only experience its frustration from a helpless standpoint, and demand a party to blame as a release, and a party to provide a cure. Hence they become easy prey for fascistic manipulation. It is at this point that fascistic political parties and dictators begin to seriously develop by offering simplistic answers which might, in better times, not be taken too seriously. The standard 'answers' are: a return to law and order; the need to restore the strength of the family; recovery of national honor; a return to God and morality; and punishment of the scapegoat conveniently held to blame for it all. All but the last are actually nothing but code words for a simplistic return to the way things were. The promise of a full scale recovery of the economy is also an absolutely necessary pledge, yet in all the emotional passion of the family, God and flag issues, few are concerned with the increase in armaments, police, military, economic imperialism and industrial exploitation needed to quickly produce such a recovery.

These new social programs are inevitably accompanied by an onslaught of slogans, symbols and clichés which often combine scapegoating with highly simplistic answers to complicated problems, all appealing to the unconscious emotional needs of the masses, and thus, serving as subliminal methods of control. These subtle methods, easily transmitted via television, church pulpits and in the schools, are a very effective way of gaining control over the psychic energy of the masses, especially when the populace's psychic energies are already frustrated, and searching for an outlet or release from personal responsibility.

Since the authoritarian individual's belief in external powers, whether it be Hitler, Nixon or the Pope, is rooted in feelings of self doubt, it is compensated for by a stubborn faith in that power, even if it is irrational. The actions of an authoritarian, done in the name of some external concept, are compulsive and often fanatical. Years of conditioning tend to produce a chronic anxiety in the individual which thwarts life-loving and life-supporting attitudes, often resulting in such frustrated demands for release that the only effective outlet is found in destructiveness towards the self and others. In short, the authoritarian ideology and behavior patterns are life-negating from the cradle on, nurturing individuals who are, in extreme and under the right social conditions, programmed to self destruct upon command.

In defense of the middle class, it should be stated that it is in the interest of the upper class to manipulate, control and keep the middle class in its precarious position, caught in a predicament made to appear beyond their control. The lower, or working class, of course, is also enslaved by the ruling class, the only difference being that they are usually more aware of their enslavement. When on an assembly line for eight hours a day it becomes painfully clear that it is going to take an extremely long time to ever get substantially ahead in the game.

The venerated upward mobility struggle towards wealth, power and happiness is not only a hopeless venture for most people, but a goal that is beginning to be questioned by more and more individuals. Contrary to what most of us have been led to believe, owning a golf cart and a trash masher does not necessarily give one a sense of inner strength, happiness or personal power. Unfortunately, however, there are multitudes in our society who firmly believe in the myth of personal success and happiness through consumer materialism. Indeed, there is a larger working class in our society than is usually noted, people who are working night and day not to fulfill any objective sense of basic need, but to fulfill a perverted sense of material need which has successfully pre-empted any other conception of happiness. This very much includes the middle class which is, contrary to all its illusions of manufactured distinctions, simply a working class which still believes in Hollywood miracles.

MYSTICISM

Authoritarianism and the need for an alienated sense of 'transcendence' are visible in many of today's spiritual movements, very similar to those in Germany in the 1920's. Such movements, both then and now, can be seen as an outgrowth of a genuine and tremendous spiritual longing in the population, an almost desperate search for a new direction and meaning to life. When a society goes through the insecurity of a great deal of social change, there inevitably follows a revival of religiousness in all its divergent forms.

Depending upon the 'Weltanschauung' of the individual, the form that this spiritual revival takes can come in the more traditional package of Christian Fundamentalism, with its Bible circles, sermons of fire and brimstone and 'Jesus saves', or the more youthful alternatives of Eastern religious sects, gurus, prophets, occult and ancient esoteric knowledge. While the more traditional religiousness tends to merge with movements upholding the sanctity of the patriarchal family and the flag, the more alternative movements tend to merge with 'back to nature', organic living and holistic health lifestyles. In Germany in the 20's, as in America now, due to the incredible diversity of such movements, perhaps their only common characteristic is their generally apolitical nature. These movements are usually not fascistic when they begin, and indeed, many remain purely spiritual in nature. However, it is with the introduction of mysticism that fascistic tendencies develop, and as we shall see, mysticism in religion has a great attraction to the alienated individual.

Like Nazism, mystical spiritualism offers the idea of supreme superiority, the fulfillment of a 'transcendent destiny' through practice of the mystical experience, and the submergence of the self in a 'higher', more abstract order of the universe. Mysticism is the dreamy contemplation on ideas which seek to solve the mysteries of existence by illumination or revelation, having no foundation in active human experience. This includes solely abstract concepts of 'transcendence' which are not based upon any personal experience.

Mystical spiritualism usually includes submission to a 'master', 'guru' or priest, an irrefutable authority who has 'the knowledge', and who can also help someone else attain it and thus, realize his/her destiny. Since the adherent to mystical spiritualism usually sacrifices independence, individuality, rationality and self-assurance, an 'Ersatz' or an artificial replacement is substituted for the adherent's personal experiences and realizations. In accepting the preconceived notions of the 'master', an illusionary feeling of power can be gained through identification with a grandiose illusion of the master's greatness. The relationship of a devotee to the master is one of devotion, dedication, humility and obedience.

Unfortunately, the acceptance of the teachings or ideology of the teacher, however valid in themselves, tends to block one's own experience and invalidate anyone else's experience that may have been different. In his study of anti-democratic behavior, psychologist Morrow found that the unquestioned acceptance of religious dogma not only weakens the self, but seriously impairs intellectual strength to the point of "undermining one's confidence in human ability to understand the world in general, and render one susceptible to various forms of mysticism- especially mystical interpretations of human behavior."[14]

The greater power chosen for this attachment will have to provide a feeling of 'transcendence' to an expanded consciousness, and thus, the ideology of authoritarianism often includes abstract concepts of power. In this manner authoritarian raised individuals tend to replace their own potential inner source, which has become ineffective, with an external supernatural concept. This mystical concept is given an existence of its own and is seen as absolute, universal, or as an intrinsic part of nature. This external, attachment enables individuals to rationalize their submission to the mystical power through the ideologies of fate, the will of God, the function of the State, the order of society, or the Laws of Science. At the same time, these individuals can feel a vicarious illusion of power, an escape from facing one's own individuality and effectiveness, as well as the responsibility which this process would otherwise involve.

Mystical spiritualism displaces the real inner source of potential active relatedness, and replaces it with an illusionary concept, offering the psyche of authoritarian individuals an easy way out of their sense of ineffectiveness. Such mystical experiences can only occur when the individual's natural capacity for spontaneous feeling and relating has already been blocked, turning the individual away from open contact with the environment and preventing the open and conscious awareness of the self. This mystical 'Ersatz'(substitute) can be most destructive, for intrinsic to the meaning of the term consciousness itself, is the concept that one's consciousness can be fully developed only in the context from which it springs: the conscious process of active relatedness. When this conscious process has been blocked, yet, unconscious impulses still occur, as they must, the appearance of these feelings from within the core of the being cannot even be recognized, much less realized or fulfilled in an independent way. The 'Ersatz consciousness', or the illusionary concepts of the mystical teaching, become 'the consciousness' which has been conveniently substituted for one's own consciousness.

It must be interjected that not all spiritualism is mystical in nature. Such a non-mystical spirituality would promote a holistic approach to personal development, using self-improvement to support the individual to integrate spirit, body, mind and emotions through productive and spontaneous contact with the environment. This creates a natural flow and a growth experience within human proportions. The ego, our animal bodies, and sexual impulses are not seen as something to be destroyed or to be ashamed of. The individual as a whole can inherently experience the divine through the development, rather than negation, of the faculties of the spirit, body, mind and emotions.

Unfortunately, few spiritual disciplines emphasize so holistically the role of the individual's concrete efforts to relate directly to the existing environment, in producing the experience of personal growth towards a higher sense of consciousness. Most spiritual disciplines cannot seem to avoid the authoritarian pitfall of one's inability to 'do it one's self', while others appear to take advantage of it. The substitute goal often becomes the attainment of a totally passive and blissful experience, however oblivious and naive it may be. The same types of authoritarian personality common to politicized fascism can be found in spiritual groups which offer a mystical substitute to active relatedness: the ardent supporters who have found a solution to their ineffectiveness; those who would rather join than be alone; the elitist chosen group involved in a noble mission to save the world. Similar are the spiritual leaders who exert patriarchal control through the use of circuitous 'good and bad' arguments either in the Western context of 'saved and lost', 'heavenly and hellish', 'male and female', or the Eastern 'positivity and negativity', 'evolved and not evolved', 'yin and yang' to confront any opinion contrary to their own dogma. In the chapters on the Nazi example and organized religion, we shall see the extent to which Hitler, and various church leaders have used mysticism, and the patriarchal role of the master/father to gain control over the alienated masses. This is especially so for charismatic totalitarian leaders, like Stalin, Hitler or Mussolini, who satisfy a hunger within people to rise above, to transcend their ordinary everyday lives, to join, indentify with, and escape into something greater and more powerful.

FEAR OF THINKING AND IRRATIONALISM

Along with the authoritarian individual's deep-seated feelings of self-doubt, alienation and lack of faith in oneself, comes a deadly fear of independent thinking. Indeed, the faculties of the mind, most specifically that of questioning, is the number one enemy of fascism. As Eric Fromm states in 'Escape from Freedom', "to feel completely alone and isolated leads to mental disintegration, just as physical starvation leads to death,"[15] for the ability of the authoritarian individual to think and solve his/her own problems, to personally find a rational way to fulfill desire, has been thwarted by the deep feelings of ineffectiveness, self-alienation and anxiety. Since the child brought up in the authoritarian manner is seldom given any logical reasons why it is bad to masturbate, or incorrect to sing at the table, for the simple reason that there often are no logical reasons, the child is not encouraged to develop a world view in which rationality plays an important role. To the contrary, the child is merely trained and expected to obey without question; "Never mind and just do as you're told!" This fear of thinking is continually reinforced in our society by an educational system which psychologist T.W. Adorno found is a prime cause of political ignorance and confusion, for it "tends to discourage anything supposedly 'speculative', or which cannot be corroborated by surface findings and stated in terms of facts and figures ."[16]

Constant conditioning and repression can have the final effect of blurring, if not completely blotting out, one's innermost desires and dreams. To merely think about one's condition immediately pushes the button of anxiety, creating feelings of hopelessness, pain and alienation, for the individual has never learned to independently question the validity of the external reality. Any serious attempt to rationally understand one's situation is bound to bring up the desire to rebel against all of the conditioning, as well as the prevailing order which has created it. However, since the individual has never learned to rely on his/her own inner strength, s/he has little or no self-confidence, and consequently tends to withdraw from any serious conflict with authority. The image of rebellion is, in itself, laden with fear, for in all probability rebellion would leave the individual reliant upon his/her own devices, defenseless and alone in a hostile world without any external guidance; perhaps the most potent fear of all.

Just as the authoritarian person has learned to instinctively submit to any and all authorities, these external powers with which the person has identified, are rarely unconscious of the advantages in perpetuating this situation. These powers are not interested in promoting independent thought and action, for the end result would be self reliance. Advocating that people must independently think and act, as long as they take the responsibility for their own decisions, would enable them to soon overcome their sense of personal ineffectiveness. Since this would result in people being no longer totally dependent upon external powers, such encouragement is most certainly not in the perceived interest of the external powers.

Self doubt, however, is very often so ingrained in the authoritarian individual that any tendency towards rational thinking or questioning is blocked by unconscious anxiety. All too often the 'solution' to the dilemma, is to simply avoid the issue entirely by accepting without question the external power's ideology. This external power, for what ever its own purposes, needs only pronounce the necessity to perform any function, or to feel any attitude, and the authoritarian individual has little conscious choice but to jump at the command. A specific authority could give a rational explanation for its command, but more often than not this is unnecessary, and perhaps not in its own interest, especially if the authority's actual motive is despicable. Rather than admit a lust for more power or greed, the answer to the people would be more mystical in nature, such as to 'protect the family', 'serve the public good', or 'make the world safe for democracy'.

Not only does the alienated individual feel compelled to obey any command from superiors, but s/he tends to do so whether or not it is in his/her best interests. Even the process of ascertaining what one's own interests actually are, becomes so anxiety laden that one's interests often merely become obeying. Instead of rebelling, the emotional attachment to the external power is allowed to override any personal doubt or hesitation, for the fear of not obeying is even greater. Thus, what is lacking in individuality and personal power, is compensated for by the strength of the authority to whom one has submitted. What one's own individual situation could not provide due to the fear of ineffectiveness, and the consequences of daring to change that position, must be found in the mystical power. Such a transaction is often completed without the individual even being aware of the exact nature of what has taken place, nor the basic irrationality of it. When this transference occurs, it is also understandable that the stronger the external power's illusion of vicarious power, the stronger the attraction will be for the alienated individual.

Fascism can be seen as a means of taking collective power by appealing to the emotions of fear and insecurity, rather than to rational thinking and objective argumentation. Such irrationalism is, of course, not obvious to those who are the victims of authoritarian conditioning, which, to a certain extent, includes all of us, for it is ever present in our society. When the majority of alienated people must find others to blame, when impoverished individuals believe that they alone are to blame, and when the economically exploited thank their slave masters rather than rebel, then they are all acting in an irrational manner by contradicting their actual interests.

Most unfortunately, after sufficient conditioning, people no longer need to be forcefully suppressed, for the job has already been done. After a while, a slave no longer needs a master, for the external controls are internalized to form a self-conception as an obedient slave. In our society today, it is no longer necessary to actually put most people in chains. In a much more subtle way, people are conditioned to regard themselves as privileged and free, oblivious to the psychic chains which bind them even more effectively. It is this alienated and irrational character structure, learned by the human masses which makes authoritarian leadership and control possible, perhaps even 'necessary'.

INSTITUTIONALISM AND PROFESSIONALISM

The failure of individuals within a society to take their own power, as well as the resulting responsibility for it, has caused elaborate societal institutions to develop, ideally to help humans in their personal and collective growth by supporting this process. Over the patriarchal centuries, however, we humans have tended to make two mistakes in our zeal for institutionalization. The first is that their purpose often changes from teaching personal order and growth, to that of merely enforcing it. The second, and compounding error, is that this patriarchal sense of enforcement has become a devious concept of 'law and order' based almost single-mindedly upon material order alone. When our human sense of law defines the act of someone charging exorbitant rent to poor tenants, as merely the act of someone becoming wealthy and successful, then the original meaning of both the words 'law' and 'order' have been perverted.

It is, however, the people's perceived sense of need which creates institutions through their reliance upon them, despite the fact that the interests of these institutions often diverge from those of the individuals they are supposedly serving. Particularly when it is remembered that it is 'natural' for individuals raised in an authoritarian manner to look to the expert opinion for the answer, and it is easy to see how this reliance upon institutions can lead to over-reliance, and finally submission to institutions. Institutions, of course, can be supportive of human growth and development. An over-emphasis upon them, however, can promote and create irresponsible people; that is, irresponsible for themselves. It can often provide the easy way out for an authoritarian individual, a convenient escape. Rather than deal with the question of personal ineffectiveness, s/he can turn to the experts and professionals for the answer: "they will know what should be done, what's best for me".

40

In the past there has been a growing but unjustified reliance upon organizational structures, and their inevitable hierarchy of authorities, for 'the answers', particularly upon educational and scientific institutions, organized religion, and governmental bodies ; those whose job it is to know those things. In the process, people have tended to feel steadily less capable of understanding the dynamics of the collective processes which seem to continually entangle them. As people have given up their own personal power to act upon their environment, they have tended to see themselves as 'the little people' with attitudes of 'what should we know?' Such an attitude is very dangerous, for it denotes individuals who are easy prey for fascistic controllers. Fascist mentality is the mentality of the subjugated, the people who feel themselves to be the 'little people', and it is not accidental that all fascist dictators stem from the milieu of these self-identified 'little people'.

When there are masses of people identifying as the unfulfilled, victimized and frustrated 'little people', or what is becoming popularized as 'middle America', conditioned to irrationally and emotionally react in a fascistic manner, then a very volatile situation exists, one in which a collective release of the frustration and negativity is demanded. This is the stuff that the need for wars, concentration camps, secret police, prisons and institutions for the 'misfits' is made of.

Fascism may be, in its own way, rebellious, but it is never revolutionary. It is always reactionary, in that it invariably attempts to check or reverse the process of social change, to revert to a less complicated, idealized sense of the past and its simplicity, rather than to face the complex source of the problem and resolve it.

Because of the public's tendency to leave it all up to the experts, to prefer to take security in the illusion that someone else must be 'in charge', people have tended to forget that institutions and professionals can only help elevate the human condition. They are not, in themselves, the source of individual or collective growth and development, through the use of some magical formula. Asking institutions and professionals to be responsible for doing things which, in fact, they are incapable of doing, is a form of escapism. To conveniently avoid any personal attention to our own individual and collective problems, is merely a tactic to avoid any responsibility for the experts' 'solutions', and we should not be shocked by the consequences.

THE SIGN-POSTS OF FASCISM

The intention of this book is not only to allow us to be aware of the fascism we find around us, but also of that which is within each of us. The information thus far can be summarized in the following ten character traits of an authoritarian/fascist individual.

1. Rigid adherence to a set of primarily conventional and pre-defined values without question, resulting in moralism.

2. Submission to idealized authority.

3. Over-competitiveness and the striving for power over others; preoccupation with strong/weak, winner/looser, leader/follower dimensions.

4. Fear of independent thinking; stereotyping and a disposition to think in rigid categories.

5. Mystical escapism; fatalism and cynicism.

6. Fear of others and the need for 'enemies'.

7. Projection upon scapegoats, inability to accept failure.

8. Acceptance of a purely material definition of 'success'; classism.

9. Irrational and unconditional defense of attachment to one's family, church or state; 'my country - right or wrong.'

10. Patriarchal sex-role identification.

Since we are starting from the premise that all individuals, through our upbringing in a predominantly authoritarian society, are fascistic to a certain extent, it is most important for each of us to first look within ourselves for fascism. However, when these fascistic tendencies are magnified into societal forces, the potential danger is greatly increased. Although intrinsic to the nature of such larger, societal forces is that each individual has less control over them, it is nevertheless important that each person take the responsibility for what is done with the power s/he delegates to others. If passing the buck does not stop here, it never will, for the simple fact is that if enough people refuse to abdicate their own personal power, as well as the responsibility for it, fascism cannot exist.

As an aid in this process, the previous information can also be summarized into a few questions which can be used to discern the fascistic potential of any organization enjoying or seeking your energy.

1. How authoritarian are the leaders? Are they infallible, the only ones with the inside information?

2. Does the group have a premise, theory or dogma that must be totally accepted on faith alone? Does this result in a strongly defined set of good/bad value judgments which can be universally applied in any situation?

3. Is there conscious programming and conditioning exerted upon members without their knowledge?

4. Is independent thinking, questioning, discussion and dissention encouraged, or at least tolerated?

5. Can one ever successfully internalize what the organization has to offer, or is one eternally dependent upon it? Is it possible to make it without them?

6. Is their encouragement and/or toleration of active relatedness of a non-predefined nature?

7. Are there strict lifestyles which one must emulate, regardless of individual differences?

8. Is self-negation and loss of the ego through self-denial encouraged, or is the innate worth of the individual valued?

9. Is the patriarchal family, including strict sex roles, basic to the order of the organization?

10. Is there rigid control of desire and suppression of natural impulses?

11. To what extent are the tactics of guilt and fear used?

12. Does the group incorporate mystical concepts?

13. Are there ulterior motives which may not be immediately discernible?

14. Is there a divine destiny or super-human image accredited to the chosen few? Are there the 'saved ones' and the 'lost ones', the 'victims' and the 'villains'?

15. Do the goals include competition for the 'hearts and minds' of all people, and how does this relate to gaining material wealth and power?

II

NAZI GERMANY AS AN EXAMPLE OF FASCISM

I n discussing fascism in Nazi Germany, it is imperative to understand that it is not the author's intention to identify fascism solely with Nazism. Fascism did not suddenly appear with the rise of Hitler, nor did it disappear with his defeat. Rather, Hitler was an extreme example of the fascistic manipulations of countless dictators and oppressive governing systems before and after; a major difference being that he had the first trappings of modern technology. Hitler was defeated, yet fascism was not. It merely shifted centers, changing the external poles of fascistic centralized power. Stalinist Russia was hardly a bastion of freedom, having used tactics no less brutal than those of Hitler. The Soviet Union was and Russia is, by no means, the sole representative of authoritarianism. Such tactics are intrinsic to the establishment of any powerful empire, as we shall see demonstrated in the development of the American economic empire. This can also be seen in the case of England, which, although seriously reduced, is still the center of a vast old empire that conquered and enslaved countries not only as close as Ireland, but complete continents across the oceans as well.

Nazism is used here as a learning model in order to apply the knowledge of fascism learned so far. Nazism is used specifically because it is currently the most complete historical example, one which allows us to trace fascistic societal development through its entire cycle. To put the evolution of German fascism into historical perspective, it is necessary to go back to the First German Empire, or the Holy Roman Empire.

After the demise of the Roman Empire, the Holy Roman Empire was founded in 800 A.D. by Karl The Great, or Charlemagne, a huge and powerful empire constituting all of central Europe, including modern Germany, Holland, Belgium, Czechoslovakia, Switzerland, Austria, Alsace-Lorraine, as well as parts of France, Italy and the Papal States. The capital of the empire was in Aachen, near Bonn in present-day Western Germany. Despite the division of the empire upon the death of Karl The Great by his three sons, his grandson Lewis The German, reunited the eastern two-thirds, leaving out the western portion of his cousin, which would later become France. Other than the Papal States, and a number of ethnic minorities, the empire was basically German; the linguistic boundaries at this time were quite different then they are today. During this period of history, there was no concept of such separate countries as modern Germany, Holland, Czechoslovakia, Switzerland or Austria; there was merely 'The Empire'. The extensive trade routes of the powerful Hanseatic League, and the Medici and Fugger families, created a potent economic basis for The Empire, controlling a large portion of European trade.

The fate of this First German Empire was cast when The Thirty Years War broke out, beginning as a religious war between the Protestants and Catholics. As all wars, it soon became political and economic. It did not take long before foreign powers began to interfere, adding large Swedish and French armies to the already chaotic situation in Central Europe. Cardinal Richelieu, effectively the ruler of France, was bent upon the destruction of the Germanic Empire in the interests of his own empire. As a Catholic Cardinal, his troops joined the Catholics in Central Europe until it looked as though the Catholics would win, at which point he changed sides, to fight with the Protestants against Rome in exchange for Alsace. Thus, it can be seen that it was Richelieu's intention to continue the destruction of Central Europe as long as possible. The war ravaged throughout Central Europe, extensively destroying the cities and country-side, devastating the structure and resources of The Empire, and killing up to one-half of the population. After thirty years of chaos and destruction, the war ended in a stalemate, with neither the Protestants nor the Catholics winning a concise victory. The only definitive outcome was that The Empire had, indeed, fallen.

After the Thirty Years War, the Treaty of Westphalia in 1648, left Central Europe divided into hundreds of small, independent states, duchies, kingdoms and principalities. In the treaty, these newly formed nations were forbidden to use the same currency, form trade or customs unions, or share anything in common that could lead to a centralization of power. This made them easily conquerable, and, as such, these many little countries were to serve as a buffer zone between France, Russia and other major European powers, providing a convenient theatre for war, intrigue and manipulation. The devastation brought upon Germany by this war so crippled her population and resources in general, that it took over two hundred years for her to recover. During this period, attempts at reunification were thwarted by the intervention of either France and Russia, or Prussia and Austria, the two largest of the German states, each vying for control of Central Europe. The Germanic Confederation was the only feeble and totally unsuccessful attempt at any sort of unification during this period.

The desire for unification, however frustrated, did not disappear, particularly since France, England and the other major European powers were reaping the profits of world colonial empires. In the middle of the Nineteenth Century, the Grossdeutsch-Kleindeutsch, or the greater or smaller Germany controversy, developed as primarily a domestic question as to whether Vienna (Austria) or Berlin (Prussia) would take the leading role in unifying Germany. This became the central issue of heated debates in the Frankfurt Parliament, a body attended by delegates from all the German speaking countries in an attempt to form a unification on the basis of a representative government. Even though this was the most heroic of the attempts at unification, it was nonetheless infiltrated, blocked and disbursed by the larger European powers. However less democratically, the domestic question was finally settled by the defeat of Austria in the Austro-Prussian War of 1866.

The German state, as we know it, did not come into existence until 1871, when Otto von Bismarck, a dynamic and powerful Prussian statesperson, forced the issue in favor of a Prussian dominated 'smaller Germany' by omitting Austria from the union. Bismarck rose to power to fulfill and represent the collective desire for unity in the many Germanys, declaring that now, after so many setbacks, unification could only succeed through the use of force 'might makes right' or 'the end justifies the means' were descriptive of the hardnosed 'Realpolitik' of Bismarck. In view of the experiences of the many Germanys in the last two centuries, and with the example of the powerful English, French and Spanish world empires, this type of thinking seemed not only justified, but the only rational way to unification. Bismarck believed, and understandably so, that the defeat of France was necessary before any form of German unification could take place, for France, if she could help it, would never tolerate the threat of a unified Germany. After socially embarrassing the French King, he provoked France to declare war upon Prussia. In the first 'blitzkrieg', Prussia quickly defeated France, took back Alsace-Lorraine, and declared the unification of The Second German Empire in the palace of Versailles.

Thus, yet another authoritarian empire, founded and ruled by the force of might, came into the political arena of Europe. A Germany which, as Kaiser Wilhelm put it, was "demanding its rightful place under the sun." The older European empires eyed

Berlin with suspicion and distrust, thinking that a powerful empire in the heart of Europe would upset the balance of power, which is exactly what happened. Bismarck's Germany was a large territory which was heavily populated, highly industrialized, and economically rich. This understandable fear of German economic power on the part of the other European powers, along with the equal fear and paranoia on the part of Germany, that she was being alienated and encircled, led to the mutual political and economic intrigue which, along with the usual armaments race, resulted in World War I and the defeat of the Second Reich, or German Empire.

The Treaty of Versailles which ended World War I was the first of its kind in European history. It held Germany totally responsible for the causes of the war, doled out heavy reparation penalties, imposed severe economic and political restrictions, and provided for the loss of extensive German territory and population.

Although it is documented that the German Government had equally sinister and Machiavellian ambitions which were thwarted by its loss of the war, and although it is certainly not the author's intention to justify the acts of any of the governments involved, it is important to separate the powerful German economic and political interests from the motivations of the German people themselves. The masses of people in any of the countries involved in World War I, undoubtedly had little idea of what was actually at stake: a global struggle for the authoritarian control of economic interests, and the preservation of existing world empires. Instead, the typical citizen of each country could only perceive a narrow picture from what was patriotically fed to them. From such a limited world view, few could gain an objective analysis, and the perspective of the German people was no less limited. An understanding of the average German citizen's conception of what transpired at the end of World War I, is of critical importance to an understanding of what later produced Nazism, for World War II can be considered as merely the second chapter of World War I.

From this perspective, the German people saw their country's "demand for its rightful place under the sun" crushed. This served to further frustrate and aggravate the smoldering sore of German unity and national pride, and left large portions of the populace feeling grossly humiliated and suppressed by the other major powers. Although the reparations and other economic penalties could and would be overcome, the territorial losses would remain an emotional issue which was vital to the later manipulation of public opinion by the Nazis. Not only did Germany lose her few recently acquired overseas colonies, but major portions of her European territory as well, such as parts of Prussia and all of Alsace-Lorraine. In addition, her major ally, and the other German empire, Austria, was completely demolished and partitioned. Excluded by these imposed boundaries were over twelve million German speaking people.

It must be remembered that in such long-populated and congested areas as Central Europe, few uncontested claims can be laid by any people to some territories due to the many centuries of migration and conquest. Any repartitioning was bound to antagonize someone, and it was the Germans who had lost the war, and therefore had the least to say about it. Although there were, no doubt, many opposing perspectives, that of the German's was that their country was once again being dismantled.

This repartitioning from the perspective of the masses of the German people, was leaving out large areas populated by ethnic Germans. In order to create a 'Polish Corridor' and give Poland access to the Baltic Sea, a portion of Prussia containing a large population of German nationals, was given to Poland. Unfortunate details of this transaction were that East Prussia became separated from the rest of the country, and the German city of Danzig, an old Hanseatic city, became a virtual island amid the new Polish coast. The dismantling of Germany's close ally, the Austro-Hungarian Empire, left the Sudetenland, part of former Bohemia, and heavily populated by ethnic Germans, along her border with the newly created country of Czechoslovakia. There was also the loss of territory in the west. Despite the fact that the pre-war German government may have had equally devious plans for France, the tangible fact was, that France, as in the time of Napoleon, now attempted to make the Rhine her eastern border. Thus Alsace-Lorraine, along with the major Rhine port of Strasburg, was directly annexed, and the Rhineland as far as Cologne was occupied by France until Hitler later took it back. Alsace-Lorraine had a largely indigenous German-speaking population, and was generally considered as part of the traditional German homeland, not to mention the Rhineland itself.

One of the few outlets for the German people's frustration was upon the Social Democrats who had staged a revolution within Germany prior to the close of the war. Although their 'November Revolution' forced the abdication of the Kaiser, and replaced the monarchy with a leftist socialist government which demanded amnesty and an end to the war, the revolution did not seem to have any great effect upon the outcome of the Versailles Treaty. Large portions of the populace felt that the Social Democrats were traitors, particularly since their government had little alternative but to lose face and accept the outcome of the treaty as best it could. This smoldering resentment would also be most effectively utilized later by the Nazis, for the government which Hitler toppled, the Weimar Republic, had been, in their eyes, founded by these 'leftist traitors'.

Despite these difficulties, however, the Weimar Republic ushered in a new spirit for the German people. The monarchy had toppled, and the old social order had fallen from grace, having been proved corrupt, ineffective and out of date. The Weimar Republic was a democracy, one which many scholars have described as one of the purest forms of liberal democracy ever to exist. In reaction to all this change, there came a genuine longing and search for a 'new way'. The youth were idealistic, humane and highly progressive exponents of a utopian counter-culture, and internationalist thinking. The last stronghold of the middle class, the family, had seriously been shattered. In post-war Germany, more than in any other country, the authority of the father and the old middle class morality rapidly weakened. The younger generation did as they pleased, caring little for the approval of their parents.[17]

This break in the old order unleashed a wide variety of exploration and experimentation. There was a lively rebirth of the liberation movements begun in the 1880's.[18] The women's liberation and gay liberation movements became effectively organized as social forces which have only recently been duplicated. In 1919, when the Weimar Assembly elections took place, forty-one women deputies were elected as almost ten percent of the entire membership.[19] Many new political parties were organized during this period, leaving the representation in the parliament closely resembling a patch work quilt.

This diversity in politics was equally matched on other social levels. Many new spiritual groups, teachings, gurus, masters and an influx of Eastern philosophies in general, became common place among many who strove to create the new, along with communal living, drugs and sexual permissiveness. This frantic search for a new meaning to life, plus the economic chaos in Germany, created a general atmosphere which was not only open and liberating, but could also be seen as confusing and frantic, at times even bordering upon general hysteria.

The cultural and political milieu of this period effected the populace in two distinctive ways. First, there were those who, for various reasons, rejoiced at the opportunity to throw off the yoke of the past and delve into the process of creating a new, less restrictive society. Secondly, was the middle class who generally shrank back in horror when its political and economic security was threatened. The collapse of the old social and moral order seriously undermined the security of this class, which in the past had strongly identified with the monarchical order and its morality. The new-found permissiveness of the 1920's was not only shocking to the middle class, but a serious threat to its Weltanschauung. Communal living, sexual permissiveness, feminist and gay liberation movements could only be seen as a potent threat to their concept of the sacred patriarchal family.

Even more devastating to the middle class was the economic collapse and inflation which followed the loss of the war, and periodically continued throughout the 1920's. When 1929 ushered in the great world-wide depression, Germany's liberal spirit was crushed under the collapse of the global economy. Suddenly money had lost its value, the official value of the mark fluctuating constantly. At times a pound of butter cost up to a thousand marks, and bartering became a common-place sight. In the interests of the ruling class, the middle class was constantly reminded that they were bearing the burden of maintaining six million unemployed. As a result, they became radicalized to the right. As all their hard earned savings were turned into useless pieces of paper, symbolizing the demise of their already precarious economic situations, most of the middle class were left bankrupt, paranoid and demoralized. The middle class soon began acting in a reactionary manner, longing for the return of order, stability and production.

The most ardent Nazis came from this middle class, especially the lower middle class, the artisans, shopkeepers and white collar workers; what would be equivalent to 'middle America'. The lives of these people were rooted in the tradition of class hierarchy. They had a way of life based upon thrift and scarcity, often making them suspicious, petty and critical of others. In previous generations, they had compensated for their lack of prestige by identifying with the Kaiser, and looking down upon the working class. They prided themselves upon being strongly family oriented in a patriarchal way, with high moralistic ideals and a strong sense of honor and duty. As we have seen, these attitudes originated in the economic, emotional and psychological repression of their class.

At the turn of the century, however, the competition of monopolistic capitalism, ever increasing in power since the 1870s, seriously threatened the economic prosperity of the middle class. In addition, the Kaiser's forced abdication during the Social Democratic revolution increased socialist power, and boosted the status of the working class, doing away with their symbol of upper class identification, and the opportunity to look down on someone. Adding the impact of the great depression, these people, who had a weak sense of self to begin with, were made to feel increasingly inferior, alienated and frustrated. Being the product of authoritarian conditioning, they could only experience this frustration from a helpless standpoint, reacting with hatred and resentment, mixed with an intense longing for a solution to their predicament. Their feelings of ineffectiveness made them desperate for an escape, and it was this desperation of the middle class which made them willing candidates for submission to an external power. Ironically, however, the rise of the fascist state would, in effect, prove to impoverish most of the populace even more, both on material and psychological levels.

It was in the wake of this legacy of frustration and alienation that fascism began to develop as a serious political force. Amidst this societal confusion, many political factions began mobilizing. As well as the Nazi Brown Shirts, the communists and other assorted groups, including regiments of the old militia, began marching. One never knew quite what to expect around the next corner. Bavaria, in particular, became the center of scores of nationalist, right-wing, Para-military organizations, of which the National Socialists, or Nazis, were at first only an obscure group. It is also important to realize that Hitler came to represent a movement which had already developed considerably before he came along and overtook it as its sole leader in 1921.

Nazi ideology developed in order to fulfill and/or use these desires, offering a tempting appeal to the emotions of the middle class. Alone, the racist theory of national superiority gave them a focus for scapegoating in order to displace their feelings of inferiority and ineffectiveness. The need for fulfillment or direction was transferred into the Nazi mystical race theory, and national imperialism. Hitler would soon be seen as the messiah who would realize the German destiny of scientific, biological superiority, and as such, it was the noble mission of the German race to save the world and establish a new order; Hitler's order. More concretely, the Nazis offered the German people the tempting pledge of a strong reunification through the recovery of the Rhineland, and the other territories containing the millions of German nationals lost in the Versailles Treaty, along with a full recovery of the economy. Nazi anti-Semitism, anti-bolshevism, the promise of law and order, and a return to morality appealed to many groups, especially to the Protestant youth groups, Bible circles and 'Jesus movements' which abounded in Germany in the 1920's. By 1931, more than seventy percent of these Bible circles were pro-Nazi.[20]

Leaving little to chance, the Nazis became experts in using mass enchantment to gain power, staging an unbroken sequence of 'national festivities'. This stage management of public life was designed to create an impression of national community. The individual was meant to feel fused with the masses. Huge crowds attended public ceremonies and were seduced into wild ovations of patriotic performances, complete with rhetorical sermons delivered by demagogues who had an overwhelming command of the subtle intricacies of mass psychology. Spectacular mass rituals highlighted the Nazi ideology of purity of purpose, filling the masses with mystical fervor which encouraged submission, the sacrifice of the ego to Nazi 'evolutionary' ideology, the love of power, and the worship of an abstract power of racial destiny which gave them the duty to dominate others. The goal was to create an atmosphere of collective enthusiasm, a singular exaltation which seized hundreds of thousands of men, women and children with a romantic fever and mystical ecstasy which bordered upon sacred delirium.[21]

Once Nazism gained numerous followers among the middle class, it spread quickly. The working class half-hoped that National Socialism would at least bring about an increase in socialism, especially since all previous attempts had been relatively ineffective. The authoritarian character of the middle class made it easy for them to accept Nazism. The ineffectiveness, insecurity and alienation so inherent in the authoritarian structure, drove many Germans to accept Nazism in the belief that it would provide a vehicle for some sort of unity and security. It was exactly these feelings of alienation and loneliness which the Nazis exploited in every possible way. It was only after the Nazis had firmly established their political power that the corresponding fear, paranoia and negativity needed to obtain complete control began to make itself more obvious. The fascists could then afford to become overtly oppressive.

The methodology of the Nazi appeal, infiltration and effective utilization of the German youth movements is both illustrative of Nazi tactics, and central to the eventual take-over of the entire society. The younger generations were most easily influenced by the mass psychology of the Nazi appeal, and once they had been won over, these youth became a vital tool. An elaborate Nazi 'youth cult' was cultivated, juxtaposing Nazism literally with Germany's 'future'.

After World War I, the proliferation of youth groups begun at the turn of the century, increased to the point of becoming an important political factor. These youth movements, of which there were over four hundred major ones, were similar to the countless youth groups of today. They consisted primarily of the bourgeois Wandervogel (Birds of Passage), and the many socialist, communist, Protestant and Catholic youth organizations. Each group was a unique subculture attracting young people into a sociopolitical community of comradery. The Wandervogel, which elected its leaders without adult supervision, resented the monotonous routine, restraints and conventions of society, and demanded a release from the tutelage of the patriarchal home, school and system in general. The Wandervogel, along with other such groups, asserted the youth's longing to be recognized as an entity in itself, and to find an awakened sense of purpose in a society it felt had become too harsh, complex, regimented and materialistic. [22] This movement also represented a rebellion against the traditional morality, guilt and control of authoritarian society, and promoted a freer attitude towards sex, especially in regard to women and homosexuals.

Nevertheless, these same German youth, who had so emphatically repudiated the existing system, were incorporated step by step into Hitler's movement during its Kampfzeit (Time of struggle)from 1929 to 1933. This was especially true of those in the bourgeois and Protestant youth groups.[23] The Hitler Youth movement was much more organized than the others, and offered a concrete platform for matters which effected the daily lives of the youth. Unlike the other groups, the Hitler Youth was militaristic. It offered the rebellious the appeal of tumultuous political demonstrations, street violence and meeting hall battles, for they were constantly at cross-purposes with legal authorities. Quite similar to the Boy Scouts, slogans and clichés were constantly repeated, chanted and memorized; the more strongly they imprinted themselves upon the youth, the more effectively they quelled any critical objections or questions. Those of a more mature nature, who resisted Nazism upon principle, were not so easily persuaded. This is one of the reasons why intellectuals were so fiercely attacked, and older people so contemptuously brushed aside.

The remaining youth groups were slowly coerced by the Nazis into surrendering their independence, and were channeled into the Hitler Youth. Many such movements were infiltrated, blackmailed, bought-out or simply overwhelmed by the Nazis. The Nazis then incorporated many of the concepts of these groups, especially those which had the strongest appeal. Thus, the young people were lured by such alternatives to loneliness as a return to nature, organic living, communal experiences, collective solidarity and other group oriented activities. Huge summer camps were organized for the Hitler Youth, where hiking, campfires, songfests and comradeship were offered. Regular meetings, parades and endless numbers of social functions, such as midnight torch processions, were eagerly welcomed by teenagers who were only too glad to have an excuse to get away from oppressive homes. Unwittingly, they fled one nest, merely to be trapped in another. Before they could get any personal experience in independently relating to the world around them without parental control, they were swept under the influence and 'guidance' of the Hitler Youth.

Starting out as a small group of about one thousand, the National Socialists were often laughed at, and were generally seen as somewhat of a joke, particularly by the intelligentsia. At the Munich Putsch in 1924, Hitler and a number of his followers were thoroughly beaten and thrown into prison. As time went on, however, and the economy became more depressed, the National Socialists rapidly began gaining in popularity.

Indeed, the Weimar Republic did not suddenly fall apart. It was systematically destroyed through a series of thinly veiled violations of the constitution, instigated and manipulated by the new right-wing reactionary party of Hitler and its sponsors, the power-hungry monopolistic capitalists.[25] Although Hitler promised the workers the expropriation of the private means of production and protection against big business, he simultaneously promised the capitalists protection against expropriation. Without this promise to fight big business, Hitler would never have won over the middle class. Under their pressure, the Nazis had to institute anti-capitalistic measures, just as under the pressure of big business, they had to get rid of them again.[26]

Hitler originally posed as the messiah of the old middle class, promising the restriction of department stores, the break-up of capital domination, etc. These promises, however, were never fulfilled. Hitler and his gang were opportunists in both the political and economic spheres. The culmination of these deceptive tactics was Hitler's meeting in Potsdam with the heavy industrialists, including Krupp and Theissen, with whom he made elaborate agreements to obtain their support for his campaign. In effect, big business ended up backing the Nazi party in the hope that it could further harness the nation to their mutual profit; perhaps one of the few hopes to actually be fulfilled. Without this support of big industry and the half-bankrupt Junkers (the Prussian landed aristocracy), Hitler could never have gained such tremendous power. Their support, however, was rooted in their understanding of their own economic interests.

This property-owning class was confronted with a parliament in which forty percent of the deputies were socialists or communists, representing groups which were dissatisfied with the existing system. In addition, there were an increasing number of Nazi deputies who also represented a constituency which was in bitter opposition to these most powerful representatives of German capitalism. Since a majority of the parliament represented ideologies which were directed against their economic interests, the ruling class saw them as a threat, and insisted that democracy did not work.

Actually, it could be said that democracy worked too well. The parliament was a rather adequate reflection of the respective interests of the different classes of the German population, and for this very reason could no longer be reconciled with the need to preserve the privileges of big industry and the half-feudal land owners. The representatives of these privileged groups expected that Nazism would shift the emotional resentment threatening them into other channels, and at the same time, harness the nation in service of their own economic interests. This they accomplished, for Nazism proved to be detrimental to all other classes except the powerful groups of German industry. The Nazi system was the 'streamlined' version of German pre-war imperialism and it continued where the monarchy left off.[27]

Thus, the Nazis achieved the rationally impossible by successfully appearing to appeal to everyone: alone the name National Socialist Democratic Party included or alluded to a wide range of political thinking. Through a series of political elections Hitler gained a majority in the Reichstag, or parliament, an accomplishment simplified by the diversity of political parties, and factionalism within the legislature, which made it all the easier to divide, manipulate and undermine any resistance to him. The intrigue, blackmail and brutality of Hitler and his 'squads' knew no limits.

Once he had secured the firm backing of the industrialists and the middle class, as well as a majority in the Reichstag, the stage was set for the most flagrant violation of constitutional law by what was soon to become a tyranny of 'law and order'. Hitler had the Reichstag burned, blamed it conveniently upon the communists, and through 'emergency' decree, brought the literal end to the German parliament, and the figurative end to the Weimar Republic. Soon afterwards, in March 1933, he proclaimed himself ruler of The Third Reich. For millions of Germans, Hitler's government, once it had come to power, became synonymous with Germany itself. Once all other political parties had been abolished, and their leaders removed, Nazism gained an additional incentive for the loyalty of the population; when the Nazi party was Germany, any opposition meant opposition to Germany itself.

The resistance to the Nazi take-over, however, was extensive. While the gloomy shadows of expressionistic art, the decadence of Berlin cafe and cabaret society are well remembered for their reflection of the times, the strong progressive and humanist counter-culture is usually ignored. In the figure of eleven million people exterminated by the Nazi regime, it is often difficult to differentiate between those who actually may have been Jewish, homosexuals, communists and gypsies, and those who were labeled as such in order to easily get rid of potential threats. Hitler sought out the leaders of the counter culture, the political left and those with the ability to mobilize public sentiment. Many leftist members of parliament were arrested and thrown into concentration camps. A great many fled, yet after 1930 it became progressively more difficult to find a country to flee to, particularly if one actually was Jewish, homosexual, communist or a gypsy.

Once the alternative leaders were gone, most of the remaining resisters simply acquiesced, responding as people too 'liberal' to be guards at Buchenwald, or wildly scream "Heil Hitler!", yet too afraid to fight him either. Because they had so long been unconcerned with politics, they were impotent when disaster struck. Consistent with the political apathy of the time, those who potentially could have stopped him did not realize the full consequences of Hitler's rise to power, or did not want to take the risk to do so, until it was too late. Once Hitler had mobilized the alienated masses, no one could stop him.

The National Socialists also spent a great deal of energy undoing the previous work of the counter-culture; the women's movement being a good example. They bombarded the media with reactionary sex propaganda, preaching the need to preserve motherhood, the sacredness of the family, and the laws of the state and of God; the 'higher' morality.[28] In actuality, it was merely a plea to preserve the patriarchal family, the core institution of the authoritarian state. Before the Nazi take-over, the women's movement in Germany had been very extensive, and was active in its demands for equality, sexual rights, abortion and birth control. Unfortunately, however, most women knew nothing about the sociological role of the patriarchal family in a dictatorship, and lacking direction in the chaos of the early 1930's, most women panicked and went along with the security of the patriarchal family. Many were afraid of the responsibility imposed upon them by an evolutionary and revolutionary world, both of which they were unaccustomed to. Even before the alternative and leftist organizations were disbursed, they had lacked unity, and had allowed relatively small differences to prevent a united resistance to the Nazis. Most of these groups, like the greater liberal element of the society from which they stemmed, were not fully aware of how serious the Nazi threat was until it was too late. [29] By the mid-thirties, the German counter-culture was dead; all was now Hitler.

Hitler posed as the popular messiah, and became so powerful that he could claim supreme moral authority in the German nation: "Today we claim leadership of the people, that is to say, we alone are entitled to lead the people as such - the individual man and woman. We determine the conditions under which the sexes live. We fashion the child."[30] Hitler knew the importance of the family to the authoritarian structure, and hence that it was the basis of his power as well. In a proclamation before the presidential election in

1932, he stated: "The final destruction of the family would mean the end of any higher form of humanity - it is the smallest but most valuable unit in the whole structure of the state." [31]

The Fuehrer's will became equated with the natural will of the people. The appeal for solidarity: "You are nothing, your nation is everything," was a very powerful maxim which made a strong impact upon a society afflicted with mental chaos and self-alienation. [32] It absolved individuals of the necessity to make decisions and changes for themselves. Hitler's success as a charismatic savior stemmed from the authoritarian freedom-fearing psyche of the people. Although Hitler had a powerful personality, his rise to power came from the psychological needs of the masses. As for Hitler, he himself held the masses in contempt and stated candidly that "The mood of the people was always a mere discharge of what was funneled into public opinion from above."[33]

The role of Hitler as messiah and Fuehrer knew no limits. The Nazi regime's senior legal expert explained to judges of the National Socialist Judicial Association: "In any matter of consequence, think of the Fuehrer. Ask yourselves: How would the Fuehrer decide in my place? Act accordingly, and you will find yourself on a much higher plane." [34] Hitler's reluctance to marry and have children, which he expected every good German to do, was explained by the fact that 'providence' had destined him for higher things, that he must never squander his vital forces upon a woman.[35] Yet compulsive marriage was the rule in Nazi Germany. The irrational character of such thinking was further blurred by the belief that Hitler represented the 'wholesome popular sentiment', a magical formula which conveniently transcended all legal codes, and provided the totalitarian system with a pretext for whatever actions it cared to impose.

Hitler declared that the masses must be protected from the corrosive effects of intellectual instruction. His system of education was a harsh one, which left little room for the pursuit of knowledge. "A violent, masterful, dauntless, cruel younger generation - that is my aim. There must be nothing weak and tender about it... I want them to be athletic - that is the prime and paramount requirement... I want no intellectual instruction. Knowledge spells perdition to my young people... but they must learn self-command. I want them to Learn to conquer the fear of death by undergoing the severest ordeals." [36] Hitler was no friend of intellectualism, the fine arts, or any thing much other than athletics. He did, however, demand control and submission of the self, to the point of undergoing the "severest ordeals", in order to be ready for the ultimate sacrifice: dying for the nation. Indeed, the National Socialists claimed ownership of the human body by the state.[37]

To Hitler, the individual was to be sacrificed and reduced to a bit of dust: "Submit the I to the thou." Nazism praised unselfishness and taught that "in the hunt for their own happiness, people fall all the more out of heaven into hell." [38] The aim of public education under the Nazi rule was to teach the individual not to assert one's own individual selfness. "The private individual has ceased to exist, he is dead and buried."[39] As such, this fascist state had gained unlimited power through the total submission of the people to its domination.

Nazism offered the idea of a supreme superiority, the fulfillment of a transcendent destiny through the submergence of the self in an abstract, 'higher' order of the universe, an order conveniently predefined. These abstract ideas of transcendence were not based upon one's personal experience, but instead necessitated the sacrifice of individuality, independence and self-assurance. In accepting the Weltanschauung of Nazism, however, a vicarious sense of power was substituted through the identification with a grandiose illusion of powerfulness. The mystical usage of the swastika is an excellent example of this control of psychic energy on a subconscious level.

The swastika is an ancient symbol which has been used in many cultures' religious rites, from India to Middle and South America. It originally represented fertility, seen as a stylization of two intertwining bodies with the seed in the center, and thus, was symbolic of an innately personal pleasure and power. Central to the Nazi ideology of control, however, was a new usage of this symbolism; that this symbol, in itself, was so mystically powerful that it could make the enemies of Nazism shudder at the very sight of it. Thus, the symbol became mystical, in that people were trained to look to the symbol for power rather than within themselves.

The perceived 'assets' of this mystical transaction, however, were not gained without a steep cost to the individual. A person's day was totally controlled and pre-ordered in Nazi Germany. The nation functioned as one huge ordered and enslaved work machine. Everyone worked. 'Arbeit macht Frei', or 'work gives one freedom' was a favorite slogan of the Nazis. After work, one should attend meetings, or perhaps go to an organized social function latter in the evening. Never was one allowed time to direct energy towards independent growth, since that would be considered egotistical, selfish, anti-social and/or unpatriotic. Instead, one was to direct all energies toward the 'higher' cause, to continually try to emulate the superhuman image of which Hitler was manifestation. God, the Fatherland and the Fuehrer demanded the individual's total allegiance, a modification of the Holy Trinity, which was so inseparable that the three tended to merge as one.

Hitler had a Minister of Propaganda, perhaps comparable to a modern day Press Secretary, whose function was to justify the government's policies, or prepare the public for potentially controversial policies. An example was the euthanasia program which disposed of the handicapped, sickly, mentally challenged, and the otherwise 'unproductive' members of society. Euthanasia was sold as 'mercy killing' and the necessary prevention of inferior hereditary offspring. As for the concentration camps, only rumors of what went on in them reached the public. They would not have been so base as to openly accost the respectable Burghers, or middle class citizens, in the fashionable cities of Cologne, Berlin or Munich with facts on the death camps. In fact, there was not even a common German word for death camps. Rather, euphemisms were used in order not to frighten the upstanding burghers. Although Jewish, communist and gay people were, at times, publicly ridiculed, beaten and murdered, most of these offenses against humanity were carried out behind the scenes, mostly on the Polish frontier, or some other out of the way location, and mostly during war time conditions. The wholesome image of law and order in a well conducted national community was preserved at all costs. This 'law and order', as gross and brutal as it could be, was, nonetheless, presented to the public in delicate terms so as not to offend good manners or civilized ears. Deep down inside of themselves, however, everyone could sense the paranoia and violence upon which this system of law and order was based.

This fascist mentality also had an effect upon the language of the German people. The Nazis debased and ruined the German language. Words and intonations soon came into use which reflected the regimented, static, and fear oriented atmosphere which prevailed. A mode of speaking became fashionable which was arrogant, harsh and, in itself, a reflection of alienation and life-negation. Cold, technological phrases, filled with sterile, lifeless ideations and projections of hatred towards 'the others', resulted from the stark reality of fascist ideology. Equally harsh and emotionally charged were the commands hurled at everyone in reference to the need for devotion, obedience and loyalty to the Fuehrer and Fatherland. Very similar to Orwell's 1984 'doublespeak', such as empty slogans, abbreviations and acronyms filled the air, striking fear in the hearts of those who resisted, and giving those who had 'joined' a rush of vicarious power. Many other words and concepts which were not desirable to fascist ideology were allowed to fall into disuse. Many words and phrases of a humanistic nature were dropped; words showing softness or sentimentality were often considered feminine, weak, and therefore undesirable. Alone, the barking sound and highly emotional frenzy of Hitler's public speeches serve as an excellent example of the harsh, and regimented tone and pace of speaking inherent in fascism. Indeed, Nazi German would have sounded offensive, if not crude and vulgar, to the ears of Goethe and Schiller, just as it did to Hermann Hesse.

The syndrome of fear, anxiety and control became so intense that, for some, it seemed that the very walls had ears sympathetic to the S.S. In the middle of the night, dark S.S. cars would slip through the streets, suddenly stopping. There would follow a flurry of clicking heels, marching, banging on doors, and muffled screams of terror. The next morning the neighbors would discover that Mr. and Mrs. Zimmermann in apartment three had been taken away; an informer had been at work. The camps worked to death and murdered six million Jewish people, and five million others: political dissenters, working class leaders, homosexuals, gypsies, the physically and mentally challenged, Jehovah Witnesses, and any other non-conformists, the 'unproductive', and eventually some two to three million Polish and Soviet Union prisoners of war. The Holocaust was, indeed, the worst and most heinous crime of the century.

At the same time, official decrees banned all pornographic literature, and pimps found their way into the death camps as 'anti-social parasites'. Thus started the 'elimination of all degenerates'. Medically supervised brothels were established throughout the Reich, although any freelance prostitutes were condemned to the camps. If sufficient evidence to prosecute a political enemy could not be found, the Gestapo would often accuse that person of 'unnatural acts' and provide some well rehearsed youngster from a jail to 'confess' to sexual acts in exchange for release.

Nazi ideology was filled with inferences to 'the mother' as being synonymous with race and homeland. Nazi leaders often appealed to the concept of mother and family in regard to racial purity and national honor. In an excellent example of irrationality, as well as the mystical manipulation of motherhood, when asked if Jews were indeed human, Goebbels, Minister of Propaganda, answered "if somebody hits your mother in the face with a whip, are you going to say thank you? Is he human? He is not human, he is a beast! How many worse things has the Jew done to our mother Germany, and is still doing." [40]

Aside from such references to the mother and national purity, or Hitler and the Fatherland, the Nazis extensively utilized emotional appeals to sexual anxiety and frustration in their anti-Semitic, and anti-homosexual programs. For example, propaganda was printed showing pictures of young nude German boys being butchered by Jews for the supposed Jewish custom of bleeding Arian boys to drink their blood for the Passover. Other publications blamed Jews for nightclub decadence, prostitution, drug abuse and sexual perversions. As unbelievable as these accusations were, they had a strong effect upon the unconscious emotional frustrations of a sexually repressed and reactionary people. Sexual anxiety and feelings of guilt found an outlet in the fantasies of such ritual murders and 'immoral decadence'. The Nazis knew well how to manipulate the frustrated psychic energy born of guilt and sexual misery. Hitler put on spectacles which appealed to the sadomasochistic fantasies inherent within a repressed and bitter populace, with thinly disguised sexual brutality. The surrender to the Fuehrer and his ideology provided a momentary release from chronic inner tension. The fantasy of power replaced the reality of impotence; identification with brutality replaced the impulse of a more tender love.

At the same time, the Hitler Youth initiated such programs as 'The Peace Policy', officially christening the year 1938 as 'the Year of Understanding'. As yet another example of doublespeak, the actual purpose of this program was to instruct 1.25 million young people to become 'peacefully' proficient in the use of firearms. The need for defense in order to 'preserve peace' was a popularized rationalization for extensive military training, not to mention an armaments build-up, which not only antagonized other powers, but cost the taxpayers up to one-third of their taxes.

Fascism, as we have repeatedly seen, is based upon fear, guilt, self- negation and destruction. Hitler summarized the Nazi attitude and contempt for humanity in the following statement most eloquently: "The ordinary man in the streets respects nothing but brutal strength and ruthlessness - the people need wholesome fear. They want something to fear. They want someone to frighten them and make them shudderingly submissive."[41] As Charles Reich put it, "where alienation holds sway, the collective power of the people is turned back against them as a gigantic mechanism of oppression."[42] Alienated and frustrated people must find a release. They either take their frustration out on themselves, through self-negation, or they take it out on others. This is exactly what concentration camps, wars and racism are about; a release of negativity, a projected destruction upon the self and others.

In the end, fascism becomes too negative and self-destructive for humans to endure. Ultimately, negativity negates itself. There is an ancient saying which has been handed down in the oral tradition from civilizations past, and it well summarizes the fate of fascism "What had been conquered through sheer force will never endure, for force alone will never hold it." The many empires this planet has seen rise and fall through brute force, demonstrates this principle beyond a doubt. A recent study by the Brookings Institute in Washington D.C. concerning the value of the use of military force concluded that the use of force is only initially advantageous. After a short period of time, it is no longer effective, for the use of force can only postpone rather than do away with the need to constructively deal with the substantive issues which caused the conflict to begin with.[43]

III

———

FASCISM AND ORGANIZED RELIGION

As we have continually seen, each part of the social triumvirate of family, church and state exerts its influence upon the individual. Just as the patriarchal family and the authoritarian state are the predominant social orders in Western Civilization, so too is the patriarchal and authoritarian church, represented by our Judeo-Christian tradition. As in the patriarchal family and state, the energy-core of patriarchal religions is also dependent upon the negation of individual power, and it is from this source that control is drawn. The ways in which this fascist control is systematically developed through the specific use of moral control is the focus of this chapter.

Fascism, as it is commonly portrayed and believed, is the arch enemy of religion. This is, however, not at all the case. While it can be said that fascism is the antithesis of non-authoritarian religion, very few of our religions today can be classified as such. In the case of authoritarian religions, however, it would be more accurate to say that they are partners in political fascism, working hand in hand, as one great oppressive machine.

What often comes to mind as an obvious example of a patriarchal religion is the Roman Catholic Church with its infallible Pope, 'The Holy Father . The Roman Catholic Church, however, despite its power, is neither the sole representative of authoritarian religion, nor the most fascistic religious influence in America today. In fact, it would seem more probable to say that, in America, where there exists the potential danger of an increase in societal fascism in all spheres, the more likely religious source would appear to be right-wing Protestant Fundamentalism. In order to understand Protestantism in general, however, we must first take a look at the history and philosophy of the Reformation, from which it came into existence.

First, however, it is necessary to analyze the Roman Catholic Church, since it was this institution which the Reformation reacted against. After this look at Catholicism and Protestantism in general, a focus upon one of the many Protestant sects, the Unification Church of Sun Myung Moon will follow. Although the Unification Church can be considered an obscure sect, an analysis of it is included because it represents a most glaring example of the use of authoritarian principles and control. From this brief yet comprehensive analyses of the three, the implications of right-wing Protestant Fundamentalism which are included in a later chapter on 'The New Right', will become most evident.

THE ROMAN CATHOLIC CHURCH

The Pope, almost always chosen from the wealthy upper class of Italy, demands total submission, obedience and devotion from his followers. God, the Pope, and 'Holy Mother, The Church' constitute the main focal points, with the distinction between the three of them often becoming blurred. The overpowering figure of the Pope as the 'Holy Father', plus the authoritarian male domination of the clergy, the Catholic family, and Catholic ideology or dogma, confirm, beyond a doubt, the patriarchal image and character of the Roman Catholic Church. Of course, the rule of ostracizing women from the clergy, and keeping them in a subservient position in general, is standard in all patriarchal religions.

The Catholic Church is a very powerful and wealthy organization, influencing and controlling many huge corporations, countries, and classes of people, especially the working poor. The Vatican is, in itself, a very pompous and impressive display of wealth and power, seeming more appropriate as the palace of some mighty Roman Emperor, which it could well symbolize. Alone the treasury and museums of the Vatican, housing the robes and crowns of the various Popes throughout the centuries, contain a wealth that is impossible to estimate in terms of monetary value. Protected by the famous Swiss Guard, one must pay an entrance fee in order to view the splendor of these riches. A little further down from the guards stand a number of missionary nuns collecting alms for the poor in Latin America. It is indeed ironic that alms should be collected for the people of South and Central America outside of a treasury, palace and cathedral, all of which contain vast amounts of wealth taken by 'Holy Mother, The Church' from the ancient civilizations of South and Central America during their brutal conquest and Christianization.

That millions of people are gullible enough to uphold and fervently defend this organization can be attributed to the methods of control that are employed by the church. The basic tactic used, once again, is guilt, through which most of that which is pleasurable in the human experience is made to seem dirty, evil and sinful. A principle basic to all patriarchal religion is the negation, control and sublimation of human sexual needs: the banning of all natural sexual release outside of the institution of marriage, including masturbation and homosexuality; the strict control of all sexuality within the marriage, limiting it to only that which is necessary for procreation, and even then guarding against any 'unnatural' pleasure through the use of such prerequisites as the missionary position. Indeed, much of our present concept of morality, far from being of supernatural origin, results from the suppressive measures of infantile education which are continued on throughout life.

Originally, religion and sexuality were identical. If we go back to the roots of religion, we find that sex was a very integral part of the religious life. In India, Shiva Lingams are worshipped in many ancient shrines. A Lingam is a penis standing erect in the center of a vagina, symbolizing creation, climax, destruction, fertility and birth. To this day millions of pilgrims hike up to shrines and caves in the Himalayas where these stone Shiva Lingams abound. There is no shame; sex is creation, God is creation. These temples are filled with erotic sculptures, with their soft stone bodies in the most stimulating sexual positions, perhaps every position one could possible imagine. Indeed, the first art forms of divinity images were the female fertility Goddesses in Europe and these Shiva Lingams. They are the oldest religious symbols known to humanity. Since this same erotic symbolism can be found in the religious art of many other countries, such as ancient China, and in the fertility rites and coming-of-age ceremonies of most tribal religions, it can be seen that sex and the regenerative powers of nature, were always closely connected with human religiousness. This should not really be that surprising, for if religion stems from human needs and is concerned with the life process, then it is inherently bound and connected to sexuality, especially since the life-force and sexuality are so closely inter-connected.

To trace the origin of our present state of religious suppression of sexuality, we must return to the rise of patriarchy. When social organization passed from matriarchy to patriarchy, with its resulting class society, the unity of religion and sexuality underwent a split. The religious cult became the antithesis of the sexual, and with this, the cult of sexuality went out of existence. It was replaced by the brothel, underground pornography, backstairs sexuality, and was accompanied by the devaluation of women. When the sexual experience ceased to be one with the religious experience, when, instead, they became opposed to each other, religious excitation assumed a new function: that of being a substitute for the lost sexual and sensual pleasure, now no longer affirmed by society. Only this contradiction inherent in religious excitation makes the strength and tenacity of religious control understandable; the contradiction of its being, at one and the same time, anti-sexual and a substitute for sexuality.[44] Well known therapeutic studies with priests have shown that involuntary ejaculation at the height of religious ecstasy is a frequent occurance.[45] It would thus seem that the mystical religious experience is not only anti-sexual, but at the same time highly sexual.

Religious mysticism, on one level, is an unconscious orgiastic longing. Authoritarian individuals brought up in the patriarchal family and indoctrinated by a patriarchal church, develop an inner sense of helplessness. In their constant personal struggle against the 'evil instincts of the flesh', they are compelled to believe in external supernatural forces which give support and protection. Thus, is built a church filled with a mystical atmosphere: the organ, the choir, incense and the sermon delivered from the raised pulpit, all of which create psychological and physical excitation. Ideological mysticism such as the infallibility of the Pope, the meaning of The Holy Trinity, the circumstance of the Virgin Mary, and the many 'mysteries' of the Church, are accepted on faith alone.

To people who are incapable of sexual release, sexual excitation becomes something torturous and destructive. Clinical observation has shown that the desire for self-castigation, or the desire to be beaten, stems from the desire to obtain gratification without guilt.[46] Here lies the root of the ideology of passive suffering which is a part of all patriarchal religions. The martyrdom complex is by no means accidental. Alone the concept of 'original sin' leaves a mark of guilt upon the individual raised as a Catholic. Even though, innocently newborn babies have done nothing rationally to incur this sin, they are nonetheless, responsible for the burden of it. The resulting sense of helplessness and anxiety are not only implanted at an early age, but continually nurtured throughout life in the typically Christian attitude that we are all 'poor, helpless sinners'.

Originally and by its nature, sexual pleasure is that which is beautiful, natural, and a cause of happiness and fulfillment; that which links each human to the whole of humanity and nature. One needs only to look to nature itself for a most objective context of the term 'natural' sexuality, for in nature's wisdom, it appears to have covered all possibilities. After the forced split between the individual's sexual and religious urges, however, the sexual experience became seen as something debasing and 'impure'. Defenses against these natural impulses took form in obsessive concepts of cleanliness, purity and morality. Healthy sexuality, or the natural capacity to experience personal and/or mutual gratification without feelings of guilt, is critical to the individual's development of a sense of self-confidence. The individual from an authoritarian background, however, develops an artificial self-confidence based solely upon obedience, which is actually a defense against the anxiety involved in any active sexual relatedness of a spontaneous nature.

It is not accidental that the persecution of homosexuals, and all others who sexually relate in ways other than for the 'propagation of the faithful' coincides precisely with the legalization of Christianity in the year 323 A.D. The same decree issued by the Roman Emperor Constantine which made Christianity the official State religion, also provided, in regards to unconventional sexuality: "We order the statutes to arise, the laws to be aimed with an avenging sword, that these infamous persons who be guilty be subject to exquisite punishment." [47] Sexuality, including homosexuality and prostitution, were completely legal until the day Christianity became not only legal, but the State religion. Furthermore, the persecution, torture and burning of countless 'witches', homosexuals, scientists, astrologers, alchemists, 'pagans' and occultists by the Catholic Church is well known.

The feminist, gay liberation and sexual liberation movements demand a re-evaluation of sex roles, and of the patriarchal family. These movements are all direct threats to the institution of compulsive marriage and the sexual taboos which are the rule in patriarchal religions, authoritarian states, and fascism in general. Sexual anxiety is one of the main, and certainly most effective, source from which the Church draws its power. The control of sexuality, as a tool for power, is so very effective precisely because it can never be stamped out or gotten rid of, no matter how hard the individual should try. Sex is such an integral part of our biological and psychological make-up that even the total internalization of societal imposed guilt can only suppress, rather than purge, the individual of these basic human impulses. Of all things to pick, perhaps only eating, breathing or sleeping would be equally as effective.

The Catholic Church's continual opposition to birth control, masturbation, divorce, female clergy, homosexuality, pre-marital sex and prostitution, are all examples of how much effort and importance the Church puts into the control of sexuality. Since it would seem highly unlikely that the Church hierarchy could be unaware of the control and power gained by instilling this fear and guilt, thereby impeding the individual's self-power and independence, sex can be seen as a vital political tool of the Church. From this follows that a full sexual consciousness and a natural flow of sexuality, would, in effect, mean the end of much of the individual's need for external control. Natural sexuality can be seen as the deadly enemy of mystical religion; and the Church, by making sexuality the core of its dogma and influence over the masses, confirms this concept beyond a doubt.

The vow of celibacy for nuns, priests and all other members of the clergy is another example of sexual self-negation. This concept is not only peculiar to the Catholics, but is widespread in all parts of the world where patriarchy holds sway. In order to understand celibacy and its functions, it is necessary to consider its historical development. It should also be noted that the context in which the term will be used is that of an externally imposed celibacy, rather than that of a self-imposed, and cyclical abstinence for the purpose of personal balance.

In India it was believed that spiritual teachers had to conserve their sexual energy in order to transmit their knowledge. A closer look at the definition of conservation, however, is necessary to understand how self-denial through sexual negation could possibly conserve life or psychic energy. To conserve something carries the connotation of a limited supply, and that this supply must be safeguarded against depletion. In nature, life or energy flourishes and is fertile in that it gives, takes and nourishes in a free and unattached way. All of nature is a delicate balance of life giving onto life. Every living thing needs nourishment in order to grow, and this is accomplished through giving and receiving, not hoarding.

In the case of the present day individual's acceptance of an externally imposed celibacy, the dynamics are often much less conscious. Individuals who have been raised in the atmosphere sexual anxiety so typical of the patriarchal family and church, when given the opportunity, will often gladly escape to the clergy and become celibate in order to avoid personally dealing with their sexuality.

As pointed out previously, however, there are two sources of fascism: the individual's demand of external control; and the external power which can easily manipulate its dependents. The Catholic Church instituted celibacy for reasons of its own. Far from being of 'divine origin', the rule of celibacy was not imposed by the Church until The Council of Trent (1545-1568), the final act of a long history of attempts to prevent the Church's wealth from being lost to the children of the clergy. The clergy, very understandably, were concerned for the welfare of their children, and provided for them as the heirs to their estates. By imposing celibacy, the Church not only gained in earthly wealth, but also received the total energy and loyalty of its clergy, whereas before it was divided between their families and the Church.

Throughout the long history of the Roman Church's hierarchy, such economic and political opportunism has been the rule, rather than the exception. Without denigrating nor belittling the tremendous social contributions of individual Catholic nuns and clergy, it must be said that the Church hierarchy, whenever forced to chose between the interests of its parishioners and that of the ruling social interests, has chosen to serve the powers that be. The actions of the Church hierarchy in regard to fascism in Nazi

Germany is a very pertinent example. In July of 1933, the Vatican signed a protocol with the Nazis agreeing to support the National Socialists from the pulpit in exchange for the security and protection of their holdings, lands and institutions.[48]

In an edict concerning education, Hitler reflects this alliance: "Education towards a national feeling derives its greatest strength from the truths of Christianity... Faithfulness and responsibility toward Nation and Fatherland have their deepest anchoring in the Christian faith. For this reason, it will always be my highest duty to safeguard the free development of the Christian school and the Christian fundamentals of all education."[49] It should be noted that a large number of individual Catholic priests and parishioners actively opposed Hitler, and suffered the consequences. They did so, however, on their own account, without support from the Church hierarchy. After the war, the Church conveniently chose several of these people, whom they originally had not supported, and championed them as heroic figures of the 'Catholic resistance' in Nazi Germany.

Sexual repression is, by no means, the only result of authoritarian religious conditioning. The inherently irresolvable conflict produced by the Church hierarchy's torn allegiance between its own self-serving economic interests, and those of its historically impoverished parishioners, produced perhaps the only plausible ideological rationalization: toleration of misery as a sign of holiness. Passive acceptance of a worldly existence innately wrought with injustice became a 'test of faith', conditioning the individual to most conveniently sublimate strivings for happiness to a mystical 'hereafter'. Wilhelm Reich notes, "Catholicism creates structural helplessness in the masses of people so that when in need, they appeal to God instead of their own strength and self confidence."[50] The common argument that authoritarian religions serve a purpose in that they at least provide something for the masses 'to hold onto' is most dangerous; such conditioning leaves people very susceptible to any mystical external authority, particularly fascist states. As T. W. Adorno states in 'The Authoritarian Personality', "It is not accidental that Nazism arose in Southern Germany with its strong Roman Catholic tradition."[51]

Thus was set the tone of Catholic ideology, a 'Weltanschauung' glorifying self-loathing and impotent despair, and a substantive root of a great deal of the human masochism so prevalent in today's society. The vision became one of a populace of miserable and helpless sinners trudging through 'the valley of tears', cursed by original sin to the 'veil of sorrow'. The only way out is through 'the gates of heaven', and alas, the only key to the gate comes through absolute submission to Rome. Only two of the many glaring examples of this masochism is the flagellation, or self-whipping, still practiced as a devotion by some of the monastic clergy, and the fact that the central devotional object of religious ritual is the adoration of a nearly naked human figure nailed to a cross, complete with a crown of thorns and trickles of blood. Moreover, each Sunday his figure's symbolic blood is drunk and his symbolic flesh is eaten.

Christianity, however, has not always existed in the forms by which we presently know it, nor did it suddenly appear. Indeed, it is much more accurate to perceive all human religions as nothing more than the accumulated bodies of knowledge which attempt to illuminate the meaning of human existence. As such, each religion is constantly subjected to revision, reformation and restatement, and each succeeding belief is built stratum-like upon the handed down knowledge of previous orders. Even though it seldom recognizes it, The Roman Catholic Church is no exception. Its origin, in fact, can objectively be seen as that of an obscure Jewish sect. A comparative study of religions proves beyond a doubt that the Roman Church begged, borrowed and stole much of its concepts, and rituals from other religious orders of the ancient world, including the pagans. Contrary to illusions of absolute and eternal omniscience, the doctrines of the Roman Church have substantially changed over the course of many centuries. Not only has the Bible gone through countless revisions and purges, but innumerable struggles have occurred for control of the Church itself, and the honor of being the sole heir to Christ's legacy.

Gnosticism, for example, was considered a great heresy during the Ante Nicean period (4th century A.D.) of Church history. The 'fathers' of Christianity, seeing themselves as the custodians of salvation, stamped out all traces of Gnosticism and its concept of Christianity as a philosophical rather than literal code. Gnosticism was loathed by the Church because it openly sought to interpret Christ's teachings within the context of all ancient systems of spiritual wisdom. By exiling reason, the 'fathers' substituted blind faith in its place, and accomplished the first step towards the establishment of dogmatic ecclesiasticism.[52] Had the Gnostics been allowed to continue, our present day concept of Christianity might have been quite different; rather than a personality cult, it could have been seen as a holistic and ecumenical synthesis of all the great systems and teachings preceding it. The victory of the Church however, resulted in the new 'revelation' that faith would replace reason, that boundaries would be set to salvation, and that the infallibility of the Church would be held against anyone who dared to disagree. To the Gnostics, Christ's life was a key; to the Christians, it became an institution.

Instead of seeing Christ's life as an example that each human is the daughter or son of God, thereby learning to take personal power in a similar way, the masses were shown a Christ who was a personal God to be worshiped as a being vastly superior to themselves. Christianity thus became a lazy person's 'faith', an escape from personal responsibility. The entire gospel was interpreted as though the most significant lesson to be learned was that Christ died for us. Few ever consider the fact that he might have lived for us. Instead of living in the spirit of his teachings, most Christians are merely living in the shadow of his death, re-crucifying him over and over again every year. As such, Christianity took the simple personage of Christ, who taught love, self-power and the illusion of the material, and instead built around him a centralized, hierarchical structure which served only itself. Yet the inescapable fact remains that Christ himself was a radical and a revolutionary in the true sense of the words; he did not get married nor work at a job, but was a wanderer who attacked both organized religion and government, calling them hypocrites and fools.

Gnosticism conceived of salvation without the benefit of a clergy. Religion was considered a matter of internal adjustment, and the Temple or Church was taught to be within each person, as was the Kingdom of Heaven. The need for the institutionalization of religion was rendered valueless, if not dangerous. The Church, however, regarded this new order as 'economically unsound', and so the Gnostics were ruthlessly destroyed, lest they free the people from bondage to the priestcraft.[53] Such were the foundations of Christianity.

THE PROTESTANT REFORMATION

The economic development of capitalism towards the end of the Middle Ages, marked a significant change in the psychological atmosphere of human affairs. A spirit of restlessness began to pervade life, as the rise of industry and monopolistic control of capital became more evident. The Reformation was essentially a movement of the urban middle and lower classes, as well as the peasantry, who rebelled against the rise of industry and centralized economic control. This movement in opposition to industry and monopolistic capital control, is even more significant when considering the fact that the urban middle class later became the backbone of modern capitalistic development. This dichotomy of rebellion against capitalist dominance and yet ending up as the champions of it, is central to an understanding of the politics of the Reformation.

With the introduction of industrialism, the guilds in which the craftworkers shared the profits in proportion to the amount of work each did, underwent a major change. By the 15th Century, many of the shares no longer belonged to the workers, but to capitalists who did not work in the same sense themselves, paying wages to the workers instead. Along with this change, the concept of time in the modern sense began to develop. Minutes became an important commodity, and work increasingly became a supreme value. Too many holidays or breaks became considered unfortunate. The idea of 'efficiency' assumed a new role of importance as one of the highest of moral virtues. At the same time, the desire for wealth and material success became an all-absorbing passion.

Another important development was the growing role of competition. Suddenly everyone was a potential competitor. The rise of capitalism destroyed the medieval social system, and with it the stability and relative security it had offered the individual. There now ceased to be a fixed place for the individual, as all classes of society began to move. One could no longer depend upon traditional status, for everything now depended upon personal effort on the material level. Capital increasingly ceased to be a servant and was becoming a master. The individual, with everyone as a potential competitor, became isolated and threatened from all sides. Luther was a typical representative of the authoritarian character and the social groups involved in the Reformation. As a person who was pervaded by fear, inner doubt and isolation, Luther was in a very similar psychological position to the social groups in Northern Europe who rebelled against the hierarchy of the Catholic Church.

The Catholic Church held that human nature, though marred by the sin of Adam, innately strived towards good; that human will was free to desire good; that human effort could aid salvation; and, in conjunction with the sacraments of the Church, that the sinner could be saved. Luther, on the other hand, taught that human nature was innately evil, and as such, humans were powerless to change it. Only through humiliation and the destruction of individual will and pride, would God's grace descend upon humans and save them. Isolation was to be overcome by becoming an instrument in the hands of an almighty power outside of the self. Luther taught that by humiliating oneself to the utmost, by giving up every vestige of individual will, by renouncing one 's personal strength, the individual could hope to be acceptable in the eyes of

God. Luther's relationship to God was one of total submission. Thus Luther, while freeing the individual from the authority of the Catholic Church, had them submit to an even greater authority, to a God who insisted on the destruction of the individual self, and complete submission in order to be saved. Luther's faith was the conviction of being loved upon the condition of surrender, a solution which has much in common with the principle of complete submission of the individual to the fascist leader and state.[55]

Luther postulated submission to worldly authorities, such as the princes, even though he opposed the Church and the moneyed class. "Even if those in authority are evil or without faith, nevertheless the authority and its power is good and from God. God would prefer to suffer the government to exist no matter how evil, rather than allow the rabble to riot, no matter how justified they are in doing so."[56] "Nothing can be more poisonous, hurtful or devilish than a rebel."[57] This simultaneous love for the powerful and hatred of the powerless, as we have seen, is typical of the authoritarian character. How Luther managed not to see himself as a 'hateful rebel' in his rebellion against the Church is certainly interesting, and is perhaps best understood if seen simply as irrational, another trait of the authoritarian.

Calvin's theology exhibits essentially the same spirit as Luther's. He too opposed the Church, and saw religion as rooted in the powerlessness of the individual, in self-humiliation and the destruction of human pride. "Only he who despises this world can devote himself to the preparation for the future world."[58] He too denied that human will and good works could lead to salvation. However, he gave it a new twist through his doctrine of predestination, which assumed that God predestined some to be saved and others to be eternally damned. For Calvin, there were two kinds of people, those who were saved and those who were lost. This principle of the basic inequality of humans is of particular importance, since it has found its revival in various racist and fascist ideologies.

Both Calvin and Luther emphasized the need to lead a moral and virtuous life; not that one could change faith through personal efforts, but the very fact of being able to make the effort was a sign of being among the saved. One way to escape the uncertainty and hopelessness, was to develop a frantic activity and striving to do something. This is the source of the Protestant work ethic, which in essence is a desperate escape from anxiety. Material success became a sign of God's grace; material failure a sign of damnation. The compulsion to unceasing effort and work, was a psychological result of unbearable uncertainty in an entirely irrational manner. Thus, humans came to be driven to work not so much by a tangible external pressure, but by a secondary, societal imposed compulsion which had been internalized. This made them work as only a very severe master could have forced people to do in other societies. As a result, people were turned into their own slave drivers. One needs only to look around in order to observe a period in human history, as in no other time, in which humans dedicate their energies so completely to the one purpose of work and the achievement of material success.

Throughout the ages humans have created their own conceptions of God, and this is true of our civilization as well. The concept of a despotic God, who demands unrestricted power over humans and their total submission, is a projection of the middle class's own self-negation, hostility and fear. Although humility can exist without self-hatred, as can genuine demands of conscience and duty, this is not the case for the majority of modern Westerners. Up to the present, the sense of duty in religious or secular circles is colored by hostility against the self. Conscience is very often an external authority put into humans by their own hand. Humans are driven to desire and strive towards goals which they believe to be their own, yet are actually an internalization of external social demands. Many humans are driven by a harshness which deprives them pleasure and happiness, making one's whole life the atonement for some mysterious sin.[59]

Indeed, in modern society the control of capital, has become humanity's master, material success becoming an end in itself. In capitalistic economic activity, humans become cogs in the vast machine of the corporate state: rich cogs being important, poor cogs being insignificant, but always a cog to serve a purpose to which self-interest must be subordinated. Although nothing may have been further from the minds of Luther and Calvin, they actually paved the way for this readiness to submit oneself so unquestioningly to external demands. Protestantism laid the groundwork for the supremacy of such economic activities by breaking the remnants of independence through its teaching that activity must further goals which were not of the self, in the self, or for the self, but outside of the self. Once humans were ready to totally submit themselves to the glory of a God which represented neither justice, love nor compassion, they were "sufficiently prepared to accept the role of a servant to the economic machine and, eventually, a 'Fuhrer'." [60]

THE UNIFICATION CHURCH

In the East there is a long tradition of joint societal rule through religion and politics. The Reverend Sun Myung Moon is head of the Unification Church, a Korean based institution which is patronized by the Park Regime, which is in turn supported, if not founded, by the U.S. Government. Starting as an obscure and bizarre Christian sect in the 1950's, the history of Moon and his Unification Church is most interesting. He was twice imprisoned; once by the Japanese during the Korean War, and again shortly after the War for a sex scandal in which he was alleged to have been sleeping with initiates of his sect.

It was not until the Park Regime began supporting Moon and his Church, while at the same time severely suppressing other Christian religions, that Moon became a well known religious and political figure. By the time of his 1973 arrival in the U.S. on a crusade, his organization's political and economic power in Korea was of considerable significance. Soon after his arrival, Moon's power and support began to grow here as well. The goals and ideology of this Church, its blatantly authoritarian tactics, and its success at proselytizing American members, are all issues most relative and illustrative of fascistic control. Moon, referred to as 'the Father' by his followers who are themselves often referred to as 'Moonies', is the head of a church which holds the central 'spiritual' aim of unifying all Christians into one institution for the purpose of destroying 'the Godless Communists'.

The ideology of this Church is more blatantly fascistic than that of the Roman Catholic Church. The fascism inherent in the Catholic Church is often subtle and thus difficult to pin-point, for it has formed over the ages and we are, in a sense, desensitized to it. In the case of the Unification Church, however, one does not even need to read between the lines. It would seem that this Church hardly finds the need to camouflage its ambitions, or how it intends to accomplish them. Rather than proceed in the historical analysis method which has been used thus far, the sign-posts of societal fascism will be used to pose questions in order to assist the reader in the development of a natural instinct for detecting fascism.

1. How authoritarian are the leaders? Are they infallible, the only ones with the inside information?

Moon is not only 'the Father', he Is the 'Messiah', the 'Master' and 'the Lord of the Second Advent'. Moon intends to not only unify all Christians and destroy the communists and all other opposition, but then proceed to rule the world himself. In Moon's words: "Only Master can save the rest of the world—I think, I myself, am in the position of that man who understands God's will, who wants to do things for the sake of God's will—I am the only person. "[61]

2. Does the group have a premise, theory or dogma which must be totally accepted on faith alone? Does this result in a strongly defined set of good/ bad value judgments which can be universally applied to any situation?

To let Moon speak for himself, "We must have dominion over America— communism is Satan. America must come back to God—Father's words will completely cover the President of America. He will give direction to America. The time will come when my word will serve as law—I will conquer the world. Yes, conquer the world—We are going to erect the Kingdom of Heaven on earth and have our King gain the hegemony. We must have God rule over the world. My dream is to organize a Christian political party including Protestant denominations, Catholics and all other religious sects. We must have an autocratic theocracy to rule the world. So, we cannot separate the political field from the religious. Separation between religion and politics is what Satan likes most about America.[62]

3. Is there conscious programming and conditioning exerted upon members without their knowledge?

The Moonies live in communal living groups called 'the family'. They get by on little food and sleep, usually giving up biological family ties and all worldly possessions in order to save the world and bring the 'Kingdom of Heaven' to earth. They must rise daily at 5 A.M., listen to a short speech of three hours by Moon in Korean, and are then off fund-raising or recruiting converts until late at night. On the streets the Moonies are always in twos, are taught to be sympathetic to everyone, and to particularly seek out lost looking youths new to the area, perhaps with back-packs. The Moonies will identify with practically anyone in order to establish a basis for communication. Yet Moon's name and the exact nature of their purpose will not be mentioned. They are to tell each person who will listen about their wonderful community of fantastic people 'just like you', and invite the person to dinner. If the person is unfortunate enough to give a phone number, s/he will be called and re-called for months, or until the person resorts to the most emphatic verbal measures to express disinterest. If a dinner invitation is accepted, someone will be assigned to make sure that s/he is treated most warmly by everyone, and that all the necessary overtures are made. Little or nothing is left to chance or

86

spontaneity. To many, the pitch comes off as extremely phony, yet to the alienated and lonely who are the prime candidates, this approach is effective.

At the end of the dinner, the person will invariably be invited to a weekend at the country farm, complete with organic food, etc. "Get out of the city, get into nature, and relate to God and universe. You'll love it-and everyone will love you". The Moonies use a very personal approach, telling people that they are bringing love back to the world, and that they really care. "You are very important" the Moonies will-exclaim. "You are needed to make this group-this is where your potentials can be used, helping create a new world." Through such methods of positive ego reinforcement, the importance of the individual is stressed and supported. Since the farms lack little in natural splendor, the idealized version of the packaged tour continues, all of this has a very strong psychological impact upon idealistic yet naive middle class youth. For people coming out of authoritarian families, schools, religions and state, usually all four, this can be an alluring tactic. Realizing that any loss of direct contact with the perspective initiate allows for a more objective change of mind, the Moonies encourage him/her not to return home at all, not to even tell roommates or parents where they have gone. Many simply disappear.

These tactics, in fact, sound very similar to those of the Nazis, especially those of the Hitler Youth. Appealing to that portion of the youthful population which is alienated and looking for a more meaningful existence, is a very effective way of gaining followers. It also employs the powerful tactic of harnessing the enthusiasm and vigor of youth in order to enrich the organization, and make it more attractive. Another similarity is the way in which the Unification Church incorporates popular alternative concepts. The use of the communal and organic approach, plus the use of consciousness raising language, produces a very different impression than what the actual daily existence of a Moonie entails.

Ever so gradually, in well programmed stages, the bucolic nature of the new initiate's life changes. Vital to the process is the fact that the Moonies are never left alone, but are constantly reprimanded, conditioned and programmed. Their lives soon become austere, filled with work, dedication, devotion, obedience, subservience and even more work. Each fully proselytized Moonie works up to eighteen hours a day, seven days a week, each potentially bringing in many thousands of dollars a year to the organization. This work includes selling flowers or candy on the street to unsuspecting buyers, converting people, or working at a regular job which is often at a Moon owned business, though seldom identified as such. The 'work makes freedom' ethic of Nazi ideology is very much supported by the Unification Church. In equally gradual stages the inductee is made aware of Rev. Moon's existence, and a nebulous connection is made between him and the mystical creation of a new world. Few, however, learn or care to learn, of the more specific nature of the endeavor, and its larger political implications.

The success of this indoctrination is easier understood within the context of the outright conditioning, programming and exploitation of youth so widespread within our society as a whole. The youth mystique so prevalent today is largely a gimmick to capitalize upon adult anxiety concerning the natural aging process. As for the reward of youthfulness itself, it is, by and large, merely a cruel hoax. In general they have few legal rights. They are owned by their families, the state and its institutions, which can and often make their every decision. The transfer of ownership to the Unification Church is often taken in stride.

Of course, it's an old formula to get them while they are still young and impressionable, as 'you can't teach a old dog new tricks'. Moon exploits these same tactics to the ultimate; work them hard, deny them, feed upon their insecurities, have them constantly repeat and listen to choice clichés, and brainwash them while they are convinced that they are the 'chosen few' who will save the world through their dedication and service. Keep them restricted, controlled and devoid of any sense of personal power. Dominate their every thought and action, and, most importantly, expect them to appreciate it.

4. Is independent thinking, questioning and dissention encouraged, or at least tolerated?

The Unification Church does not teach its followers to be alert and free thinkers. On the contrary, Moonies are taught to fear independent thinking, and shun contact with anyone who disagrees, for they are 'agents of evil'. Other than their street solicitation, they are kept from contact with the outside world, particularly the corrosive influences of their old friends and families. It is very difficult to get to see a Moonie, and almost never without other Moonies present.

Independent thinking is considered selfish. If one is caught in one' s own thoughts, or daydreaming, the response is that one is not paying attention. Although 'mental awareness' and an 'alert mind' are popular catch-phrases, it is the Church hierarchy which chooses all subjects of concentration in achieving this state of 'mental awareness'. "We must allow God to run our lives," and to the Moonies, God and Moon are one and the same.

5. Can one ever successfully internalize what the organization has to offer, or is one eternally dependent upon it? Is it possible to make it without them?

Master speaks: " So, from this time of peak, every people or organization that goes against the Unification Church will gradually come down and die. Many people will die—those who go against our movement. And even on earth, whoever goes against you, that man must be subjugated and he will be subjugated. So now is the beginning of the physical activity. Now no one will oppose the Unification Church, except maybe communism. When all the communists die, then we, and we alone, will remain."[63]

6. Is there encouragement and/or toleration of active relatedness of a non-predefined nature?

The Moonies every action is monitored by the Master's Plan, in which any independent relatedness is closely guarded against.

7. Are there strict lifestyles which one must emulate, regardless of individual differences?

The goal of the Moonies is to become 'children of God'. This is to be accomplished through the strictest of disciplines in which the Moonies are instructed to lose their egos, and all desires of the flesh. They are to lead an obedient and subservient life in an attempt to lose all selfishness, and thereby become perfect. The possibility that they already may possess the potential to be perfect through their own efforts, is not even considered.

According to the Moonies, only Moon has that connection, and only through strict adherence to his narrow path can they ever hope to obtain it.

8. Is self-negation and loss of the ego through self-denial encouraged, or is the innate worth of individuality valued?

As just discussed, self-denial and self-negation are very much a part of the Unification Church. As to the value of individuality, the Church is quite schizophrenic and irrational. On the one hand, the worth of the individual within the structure of the Church is strongly promoted: "You must be confident that you are better than Jesus." Yet at the same time Moon also states "You have your body, but your mind is mine! I am a thinker. I am your brain."

9. Is the patriarchal family, including strict sex roles, basic to the order of the organization?

In their communal living arrangements, each group Is called a 'family' with 'parent guides' assigned to each group. Moon himself, of course, is the ' Father'. The authoritarian order of discipline and absolute obedience is ever present. Patriarchal sex roles and sexual taboos are strictly adhered to. The sexes are kept separate, sleeping in dorms respectively assigned. The 'bliss' of the married state is very strongly promoted, with mass marriage ceremonies performed by Moon himself, marrying people who have often never before met their future partner for life. Even after marriage the newly weds will sleep together and consummate the marriage, only at the command of Moon. Until that time, they continue to live separately.

10. Is there rigid control of desires and suppression of natural impulses?

For the Moonies, there is no sex unless at the command of Moon, and then only in the married state for the purpose of procreation. Any other form of human sexuality simply does not exist. All personal desires not in keeping with the Master's Plan are deemed selfish.

11. To what extent are the tactics of guilt and fear used?

Alone, the suppression of sexuality and the total subservience demanded of the Moonies is enough to create tremendous amounts of frustration, fear and guilt, through which the psychic energy of the Moonies is tapped, conditioned and controlled. Anyone who leaves the Church is 'lost', and anyone going against it will 'drastically come down and die'.

12. Does the group incorporate mystical concepts?

The suppression of basic human impulses, the individual freedom to independently think and act, plus the resulting control of an external power by means of fear and guilt, result in the individual grasping towards the mystical concept of the greatness of the external power. In order to compensate for their own personal inadequacies and ineffectiveness, there is a wholesale identification with, and attachment to Moon and his mission. Alone the forced listening to hours of Moon's speeches in Korean produces a highly mystical effect; Moon's style is a bombastic mixture of furry and evangelical zeal reminiscent of Hitler and Mussolini, particularly if the follower does not happen to have a knowledge of Korean.

Like the Nazis, Moon spares no efforts at mass enchantment. Before he arrives in a particular city, a team of Moonies enter the city in advance. This 'special acts team' mobilizes the city, making preparations which includes solicitation of the press and people of status in the community to a huge, free banquet. This banquet is usually followed by a rally staged in such gigantic arena as Yankee Stadium, again free of charge, and for which enormous sums of money are spent upon publicity alone. The total cost of a rally often runs up to one half million dollars. The rallies themselves are very similar to those of Hitler.

13. Are there ulterior motives which may not be immediately discernible?

The Unification Church goes under the guise of many different front groups, most of which deny any involvement with Moon. On looking a little deeper into the funding and owners of the organizations, however, involvement of some sort becomes clear. Usually incorporated as non-profit organizations, there is an obvious overlap in the directorships. Of the long list of organizations implicated with Noon, some are: The Creative Community Project, The New Educational Development Institute, The international Ideal City Project, Students for an Ethical Society, The Collegiate Association for the Research of Principles, The D.C. striders Club, The International Karate School, The Center for Ethical Management and Planning, The National Prayer and Fast for the Watergate Crisis, and many more.

Financially, the Unification Church enjoys a powerful position. In America, it owns huge mansions, country estates, large parcels of land, industrial holdings and businesses, as well as a daily newspaper. In Korea, the Church holds tremendous political and economic power, owning large tracts of land and many business, even a munitions factory. Moon regularly receives large donations from many influential sources. Among these patrons are some of the powerful Japanese industrialists involved in the Lockheed scandal, and the armaments race. The political implications are endless: Colonel Bo Hi Park, also from South Korea, and trained in America by the C.I.A., is the right-hand man of Moon, accompanying him at every public appearance as a guard and translator; Moon and his Church have been implicated in the

Korean bribery scandal which is said to include many major American Senators. According to a small item in The New York Times:

> "Washington - Oct. 3, 1977 - Tongsun Park, the wealthy businessman and alleged Korean intelligence agent recently indicted on charges of bribing of American officials and other violations of American law, has settled a complaint filed against him last week by the Securities and Exchange Commission. The S.E.C. announced today that Mr. Park, while neither admitting nor denying guilt, has been prohibited from further anti-fraud violations in a securities case involving the Diplomat National Bank, which has figured prominently in the Korean influence peddling scandal. Bo Hi Park, a senior aid to the Rev. Sun Myung Moon, and Spencer E. Robbins, a stockholder in the bank allegedly associated with the Moon Church, also agreed not to violate anti-fraud provisions of the securities laws, while neither admitting nor denying guilt. Last Wednesday, the S.E.C. filed a complaint in a U.S. District Court accusing the Bank, Mr. Park and three others of participating in a scheme to conceal the Bank' s true owners." [64]

Moon was also a strong supporter of Nixon, whom he declared was chosen by God as the rightful ruler of America. God, he claimed, had told him so in three separate apparitions. Powerful law firms here in America are involved with Moon, including the 'China Lobby' which helped Nixon come into power. There is, indeed, a strong case for seeing Moon as a fanatical fascist, using religion as a shield to cover covert political activities, and that he is himself being used by powerful interest groups as a tool to influence the masses.

Intellectuals are also a part of Master's Plan. Moon runs a university or seminary in Tarrytown N. Y. which he plans to expand, and runs an annual, all expenses paid convention for any noted scientists he can lure to it. To allow Moon himself to explain:

"As I see it, we invite them—they will want the students in their universities to go through this type of training. Before long, we will influence the whole of the United States by influencing the intellectuals first. We are going to use them as the basis for the political world. We have to stop the university students from developing demonstrations against the government. When our paths will be stalemated in church work we will shift and make a detour through philosophy or United Thought.

The C.I.A. people will be astounded—the C.I.A. people will know the value of what you have done here and may even promise to pay for all your travel and accommodation expenses. We'll let them know that if they wish, we can pick up very brilliant young men—and have them stay in America working for their country— they will be pleased. They will know we are strong anti-communist fighters and we can be reconcilers between the blacks and whites." [65]

In South Korea, the Moonies actually have anti-communist training camps where government workers are required to attend seminars, and peasants are bused in from all over the country to learn defense against the communists. Hitler had a similar wrath against the communists, whom he constantly used as an excuse to institute the severest of controls. The march towards victory, however, does not end with the destruction of communism. Advising his youthful followers to strive to become Senators, members of the C.I.A. or else to become wives of Senators, Moon plans the American crusade. There are already Senators in America it is believed, who quietly support Moon in his efforts against the communists.

14. Is there a divine destiny or super-human image accredited to the chosen few? Are there the 'saved' ones and the 'lost' ones, the 'victims' and the 'villains'?

Moon is the 'Lord of the Second Advent' and all who oppose him will either be subjugated or destroyed, for it is 'the will of God'.

15. Do their goals include competition for the 'hearts and minds' of all people, and how does this relate to gaining material wealth and power?

Master speaks: "I am planning to get hold of worldly wealth – all!" Moon intends to rule the world and refers to chapter twelve of the biblical revelations for proof: "And the dragon stood before the woman who was about to bear a child, that he might devour her child. When she brought it forth, she brought forth a male child. One who was to rule all the nations with a rod of iron, but her child was caught to God and his throne."

> Moon is no fool when it comes to power. He knows that in order to achieve his goals he must take economic and material power, making agreements with powerful groups such as the C. I. A., Senators, and big business. Moon again: "If the top—level leaders are united with Master, then all the people will be united with our Church. Because of this work, Master needs much money. Also, Master needs many good-looking girls—three hundred. He will assign three girls to one Senator—that means we need three hundred. Let them have a good relationship with them. One is for the election, one is for the diplomat, one is for the party. If our Girls are superior to the Senators in many ways, then the Senators will just be taken in by our members." [66]

The Moonies constantly speak of the inevitable fight between 'good and evil' in the next three years:

> "God has been waging guerrilla warfare. An all-out war has not been fought yet; but it is coming. We are pushing toward that event—a spiritual hot war. Therefore, mobile team activities are like guerrilla warfare; hitting one place, moving to another, attacking another, and moving on.

95

We don't have any home base; from one day to another we are moving.., you may have to die or be killed. Would that be all right? There may be casualties by tens of thousands, but if you are not ready to die for the cause, you cannot live and save the world... so in case of war, we have to train ourselves, for the rainy day, for the war to come, train yourselves. Sometimes you have to sleep sitting up."

The targets of this war are many: "The present United Nations must be annihilated by our power... the world is in my hand, and I will conquer and subjugate the world." This conquest of the planet earth is not to exclude anyone, including the United States:

"If teams of forty members each are stationed in each of the fifty states, that means two thousand people. In the future, in each state, four mobile units will be the ideal number—that means one hundred and sixty in each state, and in fifty states, eight thousand. If that number of members are working in fifty states, we can do anything with Senators and Congressmen; we can influence them. Even Senators representing that state will have to beg the help of our state representatives... If we can turn three states of the United States around., or if we can turn seven states of the United States to our side, then the whole United States of America will turn. Let's say there are five hundred sons and daughters like you in each state. Then we could control the government. You could determine who became Senators and who became Congressmen. From this physical point of view, you can gain no faster success than in this way." [67]

Moon says that he does not want to reveal himself too soon, as Christ did, and be similarly taken advantage of. Thus, many of his followers, not to mention the general public, are not aware of his overall goals. There has, however, been considerable controversy created by the parents of individual Moonies, some of whom have even resorted to 'kidnapping' their children in order to get them away from the Church long enough to realize what has happened to them. The service of 'deprogramming' Moonies has become a virtual profession, performed by people knowledgeable of brainwashing, as well as by other ex-Moonies themselves. Court orders of temporary conservatorship have been granted to the parents of the adult-aged children. Although these court orders were valid for only a brief and specific length of time, and for only closely monitored deprogramming, they served to fend off the other Moonies who invariably tracked down the lost member. However, the Unification Church appealed these conservatorships to the California Court of Appeals, which ruled in October of 1977, that they violated the followers freedom of religious rights. Ignoring the larger question of brainwashing, the court relied solely upon the First Amendment, stating that the regulations used by the Superior Court Judge in issuing the conservatorships to the five parents "were too vague." [68]

IV

FASCISM IN AMERICA

A nyone who reads the national media is aware that fascism abounds all over the planet. We are able to perceive the fascistic nature of measures taken in the Soviet Union, Spain, China, Argentina, Chile and Iran precisely because they are labeled as such. What one can be less aware of, however, is how widespread fascism is right here at home. Acts in other countries which are indignantly viewed by our press as 'fascistic', especially in Communist countries, are seldom viewed in the same light when they occur in America. We like to tell ourselves that the police in South Africa's Apartheid Government made use of murder and torture, while ours only make 'unfortunate mistakes'. This is a conscious rationalization which barely hides the fact that there exists in America today agents of control which are ready, and more than capable, when sufficiently threatened, to use the same tactics in order to remain in power.

As the example of the Roman Catholic Church demonstrated, fascism does not have to be blatant or even be recognized in order to exist. Indeed, we have seen that the more subtle fascism becomes, the more dangerous is the actual threat, for it becomes more difficult for individuals to consciously oppose it. Fascism in America is not going to be packaged in swastikas or other old Nazi symbols. Quite to the contrary, fascism in America, as it was to the German people in the years just preceding Hitler, is rarely recognized for what it is. Despite our illusions, the threat of an American police state is already here; it is alive, well and very powerful.

THE U.S. POLICE

The rise of an organized fascistic state cannot take place without the parallel growth of a complex control apparatus. As America, Germany did not originally have a highly centralized and federally controlled police force, or extensive secret service organizations, both of which are most vital to centralized control. It was not until shortly before the rise of Hitler, and his supporters, that special police units such as the S.A. and S.S. began developing. Slowly the existing police forces were centralized and increased in size, efficiency and power, with special tactical units added for specific tasks. The rapidly escalating police apparatus, and frequency of police repression in America is hardly accidental, and bears the need for a close examination.

Before the 1960's the police forces in the United States were, for the most part, fragmented and scattered, uncoordinated with each other, and without central planning or comprehensive strategies. In the 1960's all this began to change. The most startling increases were in the sheer number of police, and the funds generated to support them. From 1971 to 1974 spending on criminal justice jumped over from 10-1/2 billion dollars to approximately 15 billion dollars. Of this sum, over 8-1/2 billion dollars, or 57%, was spent on the police in 1974 alone, eight times what was spent ten years earlier.[69] The total number of police has increased from 579,000 in 1971, to 653,000 in 1974. By 1984, this rate of increase will leave us with 900,000 police in the U.S., which does not include the secret police forces of the F.B.I. and the C.I.A., nor the National Guard or the large military complex. It is not accidental that "while many areas of public spending have been sharply cut back in the economic crisis of the 1970's, police

100

protection remains one of the fastest growing parts of the public sector." [70]

Even more significant is the growing centralization and sophistication of the police system. For the first time in U.S. history, the Federal government has become deeply involved in the police system. Federal spending on criminal justice shot up by 62% between 1971-74, and on police in particular by about 52°%. This increase in Federal involvement has been mainly through the creation of the massive federal Law Enforcement Assistance Administration (L.E.A.A.) developed primarily to fund, centralize and increase the sophistication of police strategies. At the same time, the rise of a 'police/industrial complex' has been steadily increasing; a process through which technical developments originally created for overseas warfare, or for the space program, have been applied to the problems of domestic 'order' at home within the United States.

Two main aspects of this process, have been the various police education programs designed to give the police a new 'professional' look, and a variety of new 'tough' specialized units :special anti-riot and tactical forces, 'special weapons' teams, and highly sophisticated intelligence units. Furthermore, the U.S. has been actively exporting its police concepts, technology and personnel, to the far corners of the American empire.

The new emphasis on the police is also reflected in the popular culture of America. Today there are so many television shows, films and books dealing with the police, crime and violence, that a glamorized conception of the police is standard fare. However, contrary to the popular Hollywood-Disneyland view of America, we are in fact living under the shadow of a very threatening police state; one in which the police operate as part of a much larger control apparatus which includes the military, the National Guard, private police, the C.I.A. and the F.B.I. The history and origins of the police in America best exemplify how this present function of the police came about. The earliest form of American police lie in the Southern slave Patrols, and later in the Western Rangers and

101

Militia Companies, which developed in connection with the subordination of Native Americans and Mexicans. Another origin of the police was the night watch system, which developed in order to guard warehouses, businesses and homes.[71] The primary function of these groups was to protect the property and wealth of the emerging capitalist class. The slave patrols, for examples, were charged with maintaining discipline, catching runaway slaves and preventing slave revolts.

Until the nineteenth century, however, there was no popular demand for improved and centralized policing, since most of the people immigrating to America were fleeing exploitation, oppression and police states, or were brought here as slaves. Nonetheless, slowly the ruling interest groups increased their power. By instituting regular salaries to replace the fee-for-service policing systems, the urban elite were able to increase their control of the country. Police uniforms and paramilitary organization further differentiated the police from the rest of the population, and gave them an air of discipline and professionalism.

Industrialization increased the power of the manufacturers who took the laissez-faire position that workers were commodities to be purchased for the cheapest price. Fighting against minimum wage laws, busting unions, making sure that immigration quotas supplied a steady source of cheap labor, and pitting the various minority groups and workers against one another, were all activities engaged in by the ruling elite. The people did not, however, accept such exploitive conditions without resistance. U.S. history is filled with incidents of brutal suppression of working class, union and slave rebellions. "Resistance which threatened the property rights of the manufacturers and their political allies, was treated as 'crime' because of ruling class domination of the state and its law-making apparatus."[72] Labor union and socialist meetings were forbidden, broken up, and the leaders were arrested. Strikes were brutally put down, killing and arresting hundreds of workers. In the great railroad strike of 1877, 25 strikers were killed by the police.[73]

Control of exploited African American labor was a major impetus behind the development of modern police in Atlanta, Charlestown and New Orleans. Lynching's all over the South and border states met with police indifference, and at times direct involvement.[74]

A double standard in the law also accompanied this oppression. "Arrests for 'public disorder' became a major weapon of oppression, permitting the indiscriminate arrest, jailing and fining of workers and minority groups, such as Indians and Mexicans for behavior that went unpunished among the ruling class and their allies."[75] Vigilante action on the part of the ruling elite and their paid mercenaries has often merged with 'legitimate' police forces. In San Francisco the Vigilance Committee, a ruling class 'law and order' group, led to the organization of a 'modern' police force after they had lynched and killed all the people they wanted to get rid of.[78] Often these vigilante groups later formed the 'official' police or militia.

After becoming 'official', police officers were often paid twice or more the rate of laborers, allowing them to move into more 'respectable' neighborhoods, and foster a class identification with the upper class. Where money and ideology left off as an effective measure for controlling the loyalties of the police to the moneyed class, discipline and order took over. Well drilled in military fashion, police became more and more mindless and robot-like. Since individuals drawn to the police force are very often themselves the product of severe brutalization in the patriarchal family and class system, the police badge often becomes a legal ticket to expend this hostility through the brutalization of others. Rather than personally deal with alienation and ineffectiveness, the socially supported and glorified role of a police officer allows the individual to escape into an illusionary sense of self-power, especially for those desperately needing to externally 'prove their manhood'. As such, police officers, much as soldiers, can be seen as victims as well as agents of authoritarian brutalization.

The development of a completely centralized police system, however, was a slow process which accompanied industrial growth and the resulting social unrest. It was not until the 1920's that the federal government began to build a 'national police force', a process which was not accomplished until the Nixon Administration in the late 1960's. To understand the dynamics of this process it is necessary to consider the socio-political backdrop which accompanied this development.

The depression of the 1930's that ended in World War II, was in itself, a very destructive experience in which the potential for fascism was greatly increased in each country involved. As mentioned earlier, periods of war are opportune times for governments and their controlling interest groups to increase and centralize their powers. The police actions involved in the funneling of public hysteria into concentration camps for Japanese-Americans, and the entire post-war McCarthy era, are good examples of the growth in fascistic policies. The House of Representative's Un-American Activities Committee and the Senate's McCarthy Hearings brought the imperialistic Cold War home, and led to purges of progressive elements from organized labor, universities and the government itself. Between 1948 and 1959 there were also 43,000 strikes involving 27 million workers, all of which were met with massive police repression on the behalf of the vested interests. Furthermore, the Smith Act blatantly aimed at thought control by making it a felony to "advocate revolution" in America, and led to 110 prosecutions before it was declared unconstitutional.[77]

America emerged from World War II as the most powerful imperialist force, followed closely by the Soviet Union as the main competitor. American multi-national corporations, with the support of Washington, began to greatly increase their control of the economic resources and political structure of much of the world. The Cold War myth served the function of legitimizing American police actions in such places as Korea, Lebanon, Cuba, the Dominican Republic and Vietnam. This American involvement included technological assistance and 'advisors' in the domestic police institutions of dozens of outright fascistically ruled countries. In an attempt to prevent or postpone direct American military intervention, as would later be needed to save the Saigon regime, Police Assistance Programs were designed to improve the counter insurgency capabilities of local police forces. Despite such euphemisms as 'the first line of defense against subversion', these programs were often virtual uncontrolled experimental laboratories for the development of 'effective' police tactics and technology, and the victims were most commonly the anti -fascistic forces within the country itself. American funds have trained and supplied over one million foreign police.[78] This assistance includes vast amounts of anti-riot and other military equipment which, along with the new expertise of its most effective usage, became available on the home front as well.

Indeed, the 1960's and early 1970's have been a time of great crisis for American imperialism and authoritarianism, symbolized by the major erosion of the popular acceptance of the corporate state, and the political power which supports it. This crisis in legitimacy has been widespread both at home and abroad. Many countries have revolted from U.S. economic and political domination both directly and indirectly. Examples of this are the earlier Chinese and Korean revolutions, the Vietnamese and Cuban revolutions of the 1960's, and the most recent liberation struggles in Angola and South Africa. On a more subtle level, even the 'benign neighbor' Canada has begun to take concrete steps to prevent total American economic rule.

At home, the 1960's were marked by massive, organized social unrest: the anti-war movement growing out of a broad resistance to American imperialism in Vietnam, and the Civil Rights Movement emerging as a powerful voice of the many economically exploited minorities. Both of these threats to the vested economic interests were meet with a massive build-up of police power and severe repression. In the case of the anti-war movement, hundreds of college campuses were shut down, and thousands of students were gassed and beaten, and eleven were killed. Hundreds of thousands marched on Washington demanding an end to the war, and at times the capital itself took on the image of an armed camp more appropriate of one of America's many puppet dictatorships. The fact that the minorities would no longer remain complacent was forcefully demonstrated by the 1964 rioting of African Americans in over 100 American cities. Brutal violence on the part of the police caused the death of 43 people in Detroit, 34 in Los Angeles and 23 in Newark.[79] The seeds of the rebellion, and the continued economic exploitation of African Americans through such subtle means as planned unemployment as well as blatant discrimination, would rarely be addressed or remedied.

Unlike the Eisenhower Era in which the doubling of crime remained unnoticed, the late 1960's saw crime emerge as a major political issue. Politicians most conveniently used the issue of street crime to encourage public fear and racist attitudes, all of which served to divert the populace's attention away from more substantive issues. Street crime is an authentic issue, yet it arouses so much emotionalism that it is easily manipulated. The promise to make the streets safe once again, to establish 'law and order', is an appealing one. Indeed, Hitler used it to his advantage as well. The mere promise of 'law and order' is simplistic, however, for such 'promises' are much easier than actually dealing with the roots of the crime: human suffering and inequality. The fear of crime is also a very convenient issue for the vested interests, for it can easily be used to persuade the populace to pay for more numerous, centralized and efficient police. In reality however, this is a red herring, for not only are the police ineffective in dealing with such crimes, they have been relatively unconcerned with the protection of the lives and property of the lower middle class, much less that of the poor.

The fact remains that by far the majority of serious crime, and the most violent and socially harmful acts are committed by the government, and the wealthy rulers of the corporate economy. The murder of Vietnamese performed by the U.S. military, which exceeds the number of people killed in World War I, can hardly be outdone by domestic crime. The largest thefts in American history were carried out by the government itself against the lands of the Mexicans and Native American tribes. Alone, the act of getting rich from the ruthless exploitation of the labor of poor and oppressed people, is a crime in every sense of the word. Yet not coincidently, such crimes represent only recent footnotes in the books of law. White collar crime such as embezzlement, tax fraud and bribery result in a far greater monetary loss then petty burglary or robbery, not to mention all of the completely legal tax loop-holes and accounting schemes by which the wealthy avoid paying taxes. It must also be added that although the crimes of the privileged represent much more stolen wealth and more seriously betray the public trust, such crimes are much less severely punished.[80] Those few who end up in prison, as Watergate so well demonstrated, are interned in virtual 'country clubs' as compared to the plight of the common prisoner, and receive much shorter sentences than a poor person committed for a less severe crime.

The 'solutions' proposed by 'law and order' politicians commonly include the harsher treatment of criminals, intimidation of 'soft' judges, 'deterrents' such as the death penalty, more police with less restrictions upon their actions, and more advanced technological equipment. As well as the loss of civil liberties and increase in authoritarian control, it is interesting to note that the technological 'advances' of the police are also extremely profitable for the large corporations which produce this complex police equipment. Some of the defense contractors which relied upon the Vietnam War for a lucrative market for their products are now selling very similar items to the domestic police systems.[81] In fact, police science and technology very often drew explicit parallels between the situations in Vietnam and those in U.S. cities. [82]

This new emphasis upon strengthening and streamlining the police force was one of the most important, and certainly the most emphatic, responses of the state to the widespread challenge to its legitimacy as primarily an agent of vested economic interests.

Modern police ideology claims that since modern society is more complex and diversified, it requires more restraint and regulation.[83] This then, is intended to justify police centralization, the sacrifice of civil liberties, and a police technology race which rivals that of the Defense Department.

These rationalizations are further fostered by an emphasis upon public relations, which aims at convincing the people that the world is a terrifying jungle in which the police are our only salvation. Television further legitimizes the police by distorting on the screen what the police actually practice daily. Programs portray the police as protectors of property and moral life against the unprincipled fanatics and obviously 'just plain bad people'. It is a simplistic fantasy world of mindless stereotypes of good/bad brought to us, not coincidentally, by our 'good friends' at Alcoa Wrap. The programs rarely discuss the inhuman conditions which gave rise to the crime in the first place, nor the organized opposition. In the 1950's the 'enemy' was the 'Godless Communists', later it became the 'leftist radicals', and today it has the new twist of 'demented terrorists'. Prior to the T.V. era, of course, were the conveniently popular stereotypes of the 'savage Indians' and the 'dirty Krauts'.

There emerged from the 1960's a fairly coherent set of police strategies. On the one side, sophisticated technology and a general increase in the capacity to use force was implemented; while the other 'soft' side was based on new forms of community pacification, and attempts to sell the police to the general public. These strategies represented an attempt to streamline and mystify the repressive power of the state, not to minimize it or change its direction.

This involvement of the federal government in the police, resulted in the Law Enforcement Assistance Administration, an administrative arm of the U.S. Justice Department, which aims directly at more efficiency and central control of the police apparatus nationwide. The budget of the L.E.A.A. has increased from 63 million dollars in 1969 to over one billion dollars in 1976.

In addition, it has supplied 3 billion dollars to fund research projects and to purchase computerizing equipment and intelligence systems. The L.E.A.A. reforms have basically resulted in a reorganization of the police into an effective combat organization.

Special paramilitary tactical units have also been established, of which the Los Angeles Special Weapons and Tactics team (SWAT) is the most notorious. These units are specially trained divisions which handle high-frequency crime areas, labor disputes, riots and evictions, and is on call 24 hours a day. In effect, these forces are military units fighting a domestic war, as is indicated by the original training of SWAT members by the Marines at Camp Pendleton.[85] It is estimated that there are 1,000 SWAT-like tactic units throughout the country. Most large cities have such units or are in the process of organizing them.[86] The danger of this approach to policing is that it is based on the conception of internal warfare between the police and the people, and that the police must have whatever resources, and use whatever tactics, which are necessary for the state to win the war.

The fate of the Black Panther Party is an example of how these control functions can be unleashed against any perceived threat. Faced with attacks by the police and the Klu Klux Klan, African American communities began developing counter-police, self-protective organizations in the 1960's. This community resistance manifested in people's patrol groups such as the Black Panthers, which established a system of armed patrols in order to follow the police, prevent brutality, and inform suspects of their legal rights.[87] Other third world groups and student communities demanded legislative proposals for community control of the police. The response to these attempts at police regulation was exemplified by the siege of the Black Panther Party's Los Angeles headquarters in 1969 by SWAT forces.

Despite a well orchestrated government attempt to vilify the Panthers, including the planting of outright propaganda in the media, the jury's decision showed that the attempts to portray them as a threat to the community failed. The proceedings of the trial made it clear that the Panthers had been set up and attacked by an over-armed police assault team, for reasons which had nothing to do with public safety. As an example of this disregard for public safety, the shoot-out with the Panthers, as well as that which similarly occurred with the Symbionese Liberation Army, was conducted in the middle of an African American community with no attempt to insure its safety. The actions taken against the Panthers and the SLA were less designed to minimize violence, than to serve as an example and warning to anyone who would seriously challenge the forces of oppression. [88] The SWAT or tactical force concept is an indication of how far the police are prepared to go in the use of force. Historically, we have not seen the use of such forces since the S.A. and the S.S. forces of the right-wing movement which facilitated the rise of Hitler.

Disclosures in the wake of Watergate, have revealed massive amounts of information on the domestic surveillance activities, jointly undertaken by the C.I.A., F.B.I. and assorted local, state and federal police agencies. These are merely the tip of the iceberg, however, since these agencies are not about to disclose their most potentially controversial operations. If anything, they have moved them deeper under cover. Because of these oppressive functions, any strengthening of the powers of the police, of greater efficiency or sophistication, must be seen as contrary to the needs and interests of the majority of the people.

It is very difficult to escape the conclusion that the police were not created to serve the people, but rather to serve some parts of society at the expense of others. Sometimes this can mean that racism, sexism, economic exploitation, and military aggression are defined as worthy rather than criminal. The central function of the police is to keep the people in line, especially the workers of the corporate state, which controls the purse strings of the police, as well as that of the workers. The disproportionate number of African Americans, Mexicans, Puerto Ricans, Native Americans and Asians in our prisons is not accidental, but the direct result of racist policies. The way in which police often deal with the crime of rape is another example of this pattern, for although rape, unlike most expressions of sexism, is unlawful, it is typically treated in ways which serve to further degrade and victimize women. [89]

No 'War on Crime' can provide a truly enduring solution to the problem of crime unless it directly attacks the sources of the misery and alienation which cause it. Increasing the power of the police does not do this, but only helps to perpetuate the system which generates crime in the first place. These are band-aid measures which treat the symptoms without even touching its underlying roots. In order to create an effective solution, our whole society will have to change. No social order should be held together solely through physical coercion. Oppressive empires which control the masses of people by brute force, either by direct or indirect means, represent declining and corrupted systems. This is a problem which represents one of the major challenges of this age.

In spite of these existing conditions, things can be different. Societies can and have existed without the inequalities of wealth, work-enslavement, total competition, mutual exploitation and fear, without having a vast, repressive police, military and secret service. The Civil Rights Movement, the Watergate exposure, and the anti-war movement were able to grow in size and effectiveness despite massive police, F.B.I., C.I.A., and National Guard efforts to contain the challenge they presented. The organized opposition to 1976's Senate Bill 1, a thinly veiled congressional attempt to seriously curtail American civil liberties, also proved that an alert and organized populace can still be effective.

We must realize that the police are not monolithic or invincible, and that we do not have to rely upon them. Throughout the country, hundreds of defense committees and community organizations have formed in response to police terrorism and negligence. Communities can form their own alarm systems, escort services, rape crisis centers, and drug control projects, thereby effectively preventing a total reliance upon external agents.

The source of police brutality can be described as an illness in the people which encourages the Police to do whatever they feel is needed, because they are indispensable to the community. This public attitude is an accessory, for the police cannot act brutally without the knowledge that they can depend upon support from the community. 'Crime' is whatever the people define it to be; 'law enforcement' is whatever the people will tolerate. Every community gets the kind of crime and the kind of law enforcement it wants, and deserves. To blame the police alone for this situation is simplistic, for the people have created the police in order to escape their own personal responsibility to deal with situations—"call the police" becomes "let them take care of it", and is not much different from "wait until your father comes home!"

THE SECRET SERVICE: THE C.I.A. AND THE F.B.I.

The C.I.A. and the F.B..I. are further extensions of the authoritarian need for internal and external defenses. The function of these super-police organizations, the C.I.A. on an international basis, and the F.B.I. on the home front, is to secretly protect American interests and freedom. As we shall see, the definitions of 'interests' and 'freedom' are critical, for they are certainly not what the average American would imagine.

The C.I.A. is a huge and sinister organization, the largest and most powerful secret service on the planet, with only the Soviet K.G.B. running a close second. Hitler's secret service, in comparison, was only a rustic working model of what was to follow. The C.I.A. has 16,500 'official' employees and an annual budget of 750 million dollars, which does not include its mercenary armies, nor its large commercial subsidies. The C.I.A. also subsidizes hundreds of thousands of people all over the planet, and actually spends billions every year.[90]

Not even the American congress, much less the people, are informed on C.I.A. spending or actions, for such disclosures would "jeopardize national security." By law the C.I.A. is not accountable to congress. In order to find out to whom it is responsible to, and whose interests it is protecting, we need to take a look at its functions and operations.

As Philip Agee, an ex-C.I.A. agent, writes in his scathing book, 'Inside the Company: C.I.A. Diary':

> "In the past 25 years, the C.I.A. has been involved in plots to overthrow governments in Iran, the Sudan, Syria, Guatemala, Ecuador, Guyana, Zaire and Ghana. In Greece the C.I.A. participated in bringing in the repressive regime of the colonels. In Chile, The Company spent millions to 'destabilize' the Allende government and set up the Military Junta, which has since massacred tens of thousands of workers, students, liberals and leftists. In Indonesia in 1969, the C.I.A. was behind an even bloodier coup, the one that got rid of Bukarno and led to the slaughter of at least 500,000 and possibly 1,000,000 people. In the Dominican Republic, the C.I.A. arranged the assassination of the dictator Rafael Trujillo and later participated in the invasion that prevented the return to power of the liberal ex-president Juan Bosch. In Cuba, the C.I.A. paid for and directed the invasion that failed at the Bay of Pigs. Sometime later the C.I.A. was involved in attempts to assassinate Fidel Castro." [91]

The power of the C.I.A. has become so extensive that its operations are targeted not only against foreign affairs, but also internal affairs. Indeed, the role of the C.I.A. in the assassinations of the Kennedys as well as Martin Luther King is still under question, despite C.I.A. non-cooperation. C.I.A. internal involvement in America is, no doubt, greater than most suspect, and perhaps, dare to believe.

The role of the C.I.A. in the U.S. propaganda programs is by no means a small one, and is determined by the official division of propaganda into three general categories: white, grey, and black. White propaganda is openly acknowledged as coming from the U.S. government. Grey is attributed to non-governmental organizations and people, while black propaganda is unattributed material.

The C. I .A. is the only U.S. government agency authorized, to engage in black propaganda operations, and according to the "Grey law" of the National Security Council, other agencies must obtain prior C.I.A. approval before engaging in grey propaganda. Very often the people or vehicles using grey and black propaganda are unaware of C.I.A. sponsorship. This is purposely arranged in order to keep down the number of people who know what is going on, and thereby reduce the danger of exposing true sponsorship. As such, many editorialists, politicians and business people may produce propaganda without necessarily ever knowing who their masters are.[92]

Provocation and infiltration of leftist and 'revolutionary' organizations by agents are standard operations of the C.I.A., especially in foreign countries where American economic interests are being threatened by revolutionary anti-imperialistic forces. These undercover agents are often members of the revolutionary organizations, serving as inside informers. C.I.A. operations also include bugging homes, meeting places, tapping telephone conversations, framing leftist leaders for police arrest, publishing false propaganda attributed to revolutionaries, and utilizing goon squads to beat up and intimidate. The use of drugs for purposes of mind-control and brutality, along with other methods of torture are additional ways in which the agency terrorizes people.

The C.I.A. is one of the strongest forces promoting political repression in countries with minority regimes that serve only a privileged and powerful elite. Why is it that succeeding U.S. administrations have chosen, as in Vietnam and Chile, to back oppressive minority regimes? Why does the American government support the oppressive and fascistic military governments of Argentina, Bolivia, Brazil, Chile, Ecuador, Paraguay, Peru, Uruguay and South Africa? These are countries in which hundreds of thousands of political prisoners are being held in jails, and the torture of these prisoners is common and widely documented.

114

These countries support very fascistic doctrines that see the state as the 'supreme' organism with absolute power, in which the armed forces maintain an absolute role.

To these military politicians, the individual is a myth, people exist, in their eyes, as part of the state, to merely serve and defend it. These countries are ruled by minority wealthy ruling classes, who maintain police states in order to preserve their economic empires. In the name of 'freedom,' in defense of the 'free world,' these nations have declared an all-out war on all leftist revolutionaries, politicians and equal rights movements leaders, as well as any suspected sympathizers.

As a result, massive arrests of labor leaders, journalists, clergy, university students and professors advocating change, have been going on for years. These activities have not only been financially supported by U.S. interest groups, but the C.I.A. has directly involved itself within these countries, helping and assisting these oppressive regimes whenever and wherever it can. As Agee put it, "The key question is to pass beyond the facts of C.I.A.'s operations to the reasons they were established—which inexorably will lead to economic questions: preservation of property relations and other institutions on which rest the interests of our own wealthy and privileged minority. This, not the C.I.A. is the critical issue."[93]

On the home front, the F.B.I. has paid staff to infiltrate the left. In fact, this infiltration is so extensive that there is, in a sense, a second left, its "shadow,' so to speak. They infiltrate posing as leftists, often leading the left, helping form leftist organizations and policies. Key activists are followed, spied on and arrested whenever possible. Provocateurs are planted by the F.B.I. to promote violence and extremist activities in order to portray leftist movements as violent, dangerous and a threat to the nation, thus, moving public sentiment to oppress, imprison and murder leftist people.

The definition of what constitutes 'leftist movements' in the eyes of the FB.I. is most illuminating. Recently exposed documents listing 'dangerous persons' in the event of a 'national emergency' contain thousands of organizers of such diverse groups as Native American Indians, African Americans, Women's Liberation, Jewish anti-defamation groups, rent strike organizers, and even citizens protesting against unfair taxes; in short, anyone who can mobilize the people is 'dangerous'. These people are also among the many who are targets of domestic surveillance .[94]

These are the same tactics Hitler and his gang used to take power. Fascistic power groups, in the name of 'freedom', mold public opinion to see anyone who does not toe their narrow line as a 'leftist', and therefore dangerous maniacs who ought to be hunted down and subdued. It is only through the support and/or acquiescence of the people, however, that such manipulation can occur. Nixon was not an accident, nor was Senate Bill 1, and the sponsors which brought them to us have not given up. It is acknowledged that the Civil Rights Movement was watched in order to prevent the rise of a messiah, and it is difficult to believe that Martin Luther King's death was quite so accidental. Many of us may not feel personally threatened at the present moment. However, if we are the kind of people who would refuse to be mindless robots, controlled directly or indirectly by external forces, we must learn to take threats against others as seriously as those against ourselves.

> "When they arrested the labor leaders, I was not a labor leader. When they arrested the Communists, I was not a Communist. When they arrested the Jews, I was not a Jew. And when they arrested me, it was too late."-- Martin Niemoller, a priest in Nazi Germany.

MILITARISM

In the progression from the local police to the state and national police, to the F.B.I. and the C.I.A., the addition of a mammoth American military defense establishment should not be that surprising. As The People's Almanac notes, between 1958 and 1975, "the U.S. Government has spent over a trillion dollars on war budgets, not including the hundreds of billions for war-connected space flights, veterans' benefits, interest to the bankers on money borrowed for previous wars, etc. A trillion dollars is a thousand billion, or a million million. It's quite a bit of money."[95]

The military is merely the logical extension of the same needs and fears which created the police forces, onto the global level. From the advent of recorded history, the chief factor behind wars has always been material greed. It is this same greed which provokes some people to do anything to get it, who then must be prepared to do at least as much to keep it. The bitter irony is that these same people have always been the controlling interest groups, be they the Church, State, class or Party. The great mass of society on either side, however, is always bound to lose out, for it is the oppressed poor and near-poor who do the dirty work in a war.

The focus of this section will not be to get caught up in the external dimensions of the insanity of the acts of war itself. In any war each side can be proven to have been 'right' or 'wrong', and all sides can be proven to have been 'right' and 'wrong'. Rather, the aim is to go beyond this bickering over good and bad, to the reasons people need to choose sides and go to war at all. This will inevitably lead us to the question of how people can be convinced to go against their own needs, and effectively fight to defend the very source of their own oppression. The saying "what if they gave a war and nobody came" is not a joke for it directly uncovers a possible choice which many people have forgotten. That they have forgotten this choice, is not accidental.

We have seen that defensiveness, and the need to project self-alienation, and societal frustrations onto a scapegoat, is a convenient outlet or escape for authoritarian individuals who refuse to face their own problems, and the need for change. This becomes manifest on the societal level through the creation of THE ENEMY. Although there will always be differences of perspective and thus opinion, seeing conflict as the understandable result of the wide range of human experience, allows room for constructive communication and reconciliation. If, however, we can only see conflict in terms of 'the bad guys' and their supposedly demonic forces 'out there', always outside of ourselves, then it most conveniently allows us to become 'the good guys'. Rather than actually deal with the problems at hand, this enemy is instead blamed for all the problems. Arguments in support of military 'security' are in fact rooted in fear, paranoia and insecurity. The need for an enemy is often a self-projection of alienation and fear. As John Dewey the renowned American educator and philosopher, put so well:

> "The serious threat to our democracy is not the existence of foreign totalitarian states. It is the existence within our own personal attitudes and within our own institutions of conditions which have given a victory to external authority, discipline and uniformity. The battlefield is also accordingly here—within ourselves and our institutions."[96]

The old authoritarian consciousness of enemies, fear, guilt, greed and brute force, now threaten us with not only enslavement as in the time of Hitler, but with total destruction. This preoccupation with labels, titles, categories, divisions, borders, races, families, nations, ideologies, religions, and the perceived need to defend them all, is inherently restrictive and alienating. Citadels, walls, borders and defenses can be seen as forms of paranoid escapism, which eventually turn in on themselves. These same walls, when viewed from an external perspective, become a prison. The sad fact is that authoritarian people would rather fight wars than deal with their own and collective problems on a day-to-day basis. It is much easier to defend some abstract idea of the family, nation, and all those who are 'normal' and 'good' from a depersonalized enemy. Desperate grasping onto nationalism, ideology or dogma in a last effort to escape facing our personal shortcomings renders the saying "patriotism is the last refuge of a scoundrel" as most accurate.

American ideology postulates a national destiny through expansion of science, technology and American democracy. Like Nazism, Americanism claims superior nationality in its responsibility for world peace. American controlling interests have

118

not hesitated to play upon nationalistic sympathy, just as Hitler did by using the previously mentioned Versailles Treaty as 'proof' that the German people were being unfairly treated, a convenient diversion from the real issues at hand. By choosing and magnifying the perspective that the Versailles Treaty was unfair, Hitler was able to rally the masses behind him in a reactionary projection upon the enemy of all Germany's many internal problems.

At a time when the symbolic and actual rebellion of Third World Countries long controlled by U.S. economic, cultural and military penetration fills the daily news, the emphasis is upon the 'ingratitude' of these nations. American defeats in the United Nations are attributed to the 'third-rate petty dictatorships'; the Arab oil monopoly was instigated 'to bleed the U.S. taxpayer dry'; and any country which dares to disagree with the U.S. position is 'ungrateful for all we've done for them'. Such ploys are intentionally orchestrated to play upon the American people's desire to feel no wrong, for we are a "generous people who receive nothing but hostility in return for all of our compassionate and selfless concern to better the world."

Appeals to civic duty are also an important factor in the defensive mobilization of the people. It is by no means coincidental that, although fascism goes by other names, it is always connected to an emotional need and source in the family and State. Total and absolute obedience to the Motherland or Fatherland, where a little apple pie of motherhood is mixed with the mystical patriotism of the flag, produces a happy and smiling family of 'good' citizens marching off to the 'national destiny.' This destiny, whether it be the creation of a 'superior race' or 'making the world safe for democracy' can serve in the long run only the needs of those who manipulate the group emotions for their own gain in power and wealth. For the individual, it can only provide a temporary alienated or vicarious sense of power, providing a sense of 'destiny' or glorious purposefulness which is sadly missing in terms of individual lives.

The stability of the family and state can be seen as merely different extensions of the same need for a sense of external security, with the resultant premium upon honor, duty, obligation, pride, patriotism, and a responsibility toward both, in order to maintain the stability of these structures. Individual strength and security are replaced or compensated for by an attachment and dependence upon an over emphasis upon external organizations such as family, state, police and military.

Another devious ploy to convince people to take up arms is sexual fear and repression. Such sayings as 'the army will make a man out of you," "are you man enough to kill?", "or are you a sissy?", are only a few of the many intimidations used to promote militarism. The use of homophobia in the military is indeed ironic for an institution that structurally is very conducive to homosexual activity. What is a sissy? Someone who dares to step out of the unnatural and oppressive role of 'man'? The irrational character of the sexist roles becomes painfully clear in the obsessive need for patriarchal males to 'prove their manhood.' Why is there a need to prove masculinity? Is it perhaps that women are in comparison seen as less than men? Or is this caused by the emotional crippling of humans through the imposed, predefined and strict requirements of such impossible to achieve gender roles, that no one feels very confident? .

It is, therefore, the people who, out of their own insecurity and alienation, create the need for external protection and strength. Without a fear-oriented, self-negating society, dominated by material greed, there would never develop the need for such militarism. Yet, once created, this institution and its cultural background has the power to perpetuate itself on both the sub-conscious and conscious levels. Not only is there then a large bureaucratic class, a war industry,(the military industrial complex), and millions of jobs that depend upon militarism, but a major portion of the economy ends up being based on the military power of the nation. The more powerful the military, the larger the 'sphere of economic influence' becomes.

The fact that our economy could be based on anything else is not even considered. Rather, millions of people whose jobs depend, directly or indirectly on militarism, have a direct interest in furthering and maintaining this structure. A huge class dependant on militarism can only thrive if they feel they are needed and that war therefore, is inevitable.

Consciously maintaining high levels of unemployment, and impoverished classes of people, not only supplies a cheap source of labor, but increases the number of people who are willing to join the military, in order to have at least some kind of a job. Others join the military in order to escape oppressive home situations, and to get out into the world. Yet, the extent to which military defense has penetrated our society goes far beyond the need for jobs, and includes a large measure of public programming. The vast amount of conditioning required to create the needed supply of obedient fodder for the military starts at an early age in authoritarian societies. An excellent example of this conditioning is the organization known as the Boy Scouts. What we know as the Boy Scouts originated at the turn of the century in England as a reaction to the increased freedom and rebelliousness of the youth. Similar youth movements started in Germany at the same time, both flourishing during the 1920's and 1930's. It was from this origin that the Hitler Youth was to soon develop.

The Hitler Youth has since been destroyed, while our Boy Scouts and Girl Scouts continue on as some noble attempt to occupy, entertain and discipline the youth. Many of the same principles apply to both the Boy Scouts and the Hitler Youth, such as the need to regiment and program the youth. An example is the repetition of slogans and clichés such as: "trustworthy, loyal, obedient, cheerful, thrifty, brave, clean and reverent," which instill an authoritarian order in the youth. This, plus religious, sexual and educational programming, have the overall effect of producing obedient, patriotic, and disciplined individuals who often have lost contact with their own spontaneity, sense of self-worth and self-power.

Furthermore, the violence so prevalent on T.V. produces a child that has witnessed thousands of murders and rapes in their living room, leaving strong impressions of fear, brutalization, alienation and survival of the fittest. Indeed, today's youth brought up on T.V., with such 'entertainment' as police and military shows glorifying violence for the sake of 'peace and order,' may well be ripe for exploitation by the militaristically minded.

Militarism demands absolute obedience and regimentation of its followers. A lack of independent thinking and action, other than along preconceived patterns and roles, is not only rewarded in the military, but is a direct requirement of this institution. In order to more fully understand how this fear of independent thinking and action can become so extensive in a society, it will prove most illuminating to take a look at the standard American educational system which molds our youth.

EDUCATION

In America today, almost everyone acknowledges that there is something wrong with the educational system. College boards are dropping each year, discipline problems have increased, and drugs have even invaded rural areas.

Although little thought seems to be given to exactly what the schools are supposed to be doing, everyone seems to have an 'answer' to why they aren't doing 'it'. Parents blame teachers, teachers blame the administrators and school boards, and they in turn blame the parents. Each also blame the students who ironically enough have little, or no say at all, when it comes to the issue of what schools are supposed to be doing. Although the present problem of the unequal distribution of school funding, based only on the wealth of the school district, is a valid and important issue, the central problem in terms of fascism lies much deeper.

Throughout our study of fascism, we have repeatedly traced the external "political" process back to the failure of individuals to take their own power and the resulting responsibility for that power. Central to taking this power, is the ability for each person to perceive that within the self lies the potential to actively relate with each person, situation or issue, and come up with a workable course of action, answer or solution. At the same time, the individual can learn to relate as a whole being, unrestricted and open to an environment that is meaningful and challenging. It is this inner process that is the key to human growth and development. One would think that any societal concept of education would center around the support and nourishment of this process. This would solve the original dilemma by identifying the main purpose of organized education.

Unfortunately, however, in all but a few alternative, private and mostly upper middle class schools, the exact opposite takes place, as the student is programmed in the reverse. In our educational system, this internal process, or search for meaning and truth is not given much attention. In 'modern' thinking, truth has been made out to be a weird metaphysical concept, and something that is relative to each individual. The theory of relativity has been misconstrued to be an entirely subjective matter, a personal choice. But the fact that truth may be different for each individual, does not lessen the fact that each individual has an interest in truth, not only with regard to his/her orientation in the outer world, but also realizing that one's own strength depends, to a great extent, on one's knowing the truth about himself/herself.[97] Would it not, therefore, seem more intelligent to support the individual in this process of self-knowledge? Most experienced teachers will agree that in the end the students must 'learn' and 'do' by themselves, no one can do it for them. To 'know thyself' is to tap the source of human strength and happiness. Furthermore, if self-knowledge and truth is different for each individual, where is there room for uniformity, conformity and regimentation as we see it in our schools?

In our educational system, as well as in our society in general, the superstition prevails that by knowing more and more facts about something and everything, one arrives somehow at an awareness and knowledge of what reality is. Hundreds of scattered and unrelated facts are dumped or drilled into the heads of students. So much time and energy is spent in learning, or rather, 'memorizing' more and more facts, that there is little room left for thinking, which also includes an inward process.

In our society children are in general treated with condescension, as not to be taken seriously, in need of training and conditioning. Therefore they are not responsible to themselves, but to the authorities (parents, teachers, the state, etc.) into whose hands they are put until 'properly' trained. This insincerity and disrespect toward children not only discourages independent thinking, but also is the cause for a lot of resentment on the part of the children. A similar attitude of condescension is also directed toward the old, physically handicapped, mentally challenged, women, etc. These are forms of life- negation which deny individuals their freedom to be, simply because they have no power in the limited authoritarian sense of the word.

Since our institutions are made up of and created by the individuals of our society, they quite naturally reflect the same attitudes, values, and thinking prevalent in our society. As such, individual self knowledge, spontaneity and creativity are not supported in the existing educational system. Rather, conformity to the existing patriarchal material order prevails. Children are taught to make 'good marks', to strive to be 'successful,' 'competitive' and to be admired and popular. From the very beginning of education, original thinking is discouraged and ready- made thoughts and attitudes are put into children's heads.

Unfortunately, the result of all this conditioning, which is also supported in the general environment in every way, from T.V. to football and cheerleaders, leaves many people living under the illusion that they know what they want, while actually they want what they're supposed to want. Over the years their subconscious and consequently conscious selves have been conditioned through the combined efforts of education, advertisement, moral-attitude training, religious dogma, and civics ideologies.

This process of knowing what we really want is not as easy as most people think, but is one of the most challenging growth experiences any human being has to solve. It is a task that authoritarian individuals desperately try to avoid by accepting ready-made goals as though they were their own. This influences us from the 'career' we choose, the style of the clothes we wear, to our religious and political beliefs. In many instances, as Eric Fromm notes, "we have become automatons who live under the illusion of being self-willed individuals."[98]

The insignificance and powerlessness of the individual is increased by this suppression of spontaneous feelings, and thereby the development of genuine individuality. In our culture, education all too often results in the destruction of spontaneity, and in the substitution of original thinking by superimposed thoughts, feelings, desires and wishes. Original thought does not mean an idea that no one has thought of before, but an idea that originates in the individual as a result of his/her own activity, and has not been planted there purely by means of suggestion. The right to express our thoughts is only meaningful if we are capable of having our own thoughts. Indeed, a society can have freedom of speech on the books of law, yet have conditioned the minds of the populace to such an extent that it has become a meaningless law.

Our children are taught to be friendly at all times, smiling, cute and naive. These plus many other ways of expression become conditioned until they are automatic responses which can be turned on and off like a T.V. Any child who will not conform is subdued or broken by means of the intimidation process. The child who will not conform and therefore stands out is made fun of, ridiculed, made to feel guilty for being different, and labeled a 'problem child.' This treatment in turn creates strong feelings of guilt, fear, shyness and/or resentment in that child, and as a result, some will withdraw into themselves, while others will rebel.

Usually these "problem children" are described as "emotionally disturbed." In our culture and its educational system, emotions are in general discouraged. This is most unfortunate, since any creative thinking or activity is inseparably linked with emotion. Thus, it has become an ideal to think and live without emotions. 'Emotional' has become synonymous with being 'unsound' or 'unbalanced.' The fact has been overlooked, however, that emotions, as all things, has a full range of potential usage, but it too can exist in a balanced and healthy state, a situation which cannot be arrived at by avoiding and denying the emotional part of human development.

This denial of our emotional, sensual and animal nature is, of course, made even more frustrated by sexual negation, which we have seen weakens a person's courage for spontaneous expression in all spheres of human activity. The patriarchal sex-roles, taboos and attitudes are promoted and supported throughout our educational system. Identification with and submission to male dominance is perpetuated in the use of words such as man, he, mankind, etc., while sexual education itself, if at all dealt with, is done in a superficial way so as to get it out of the way.

One result of this emotional self-negation is the cheap and insincere sentimentality with which T.V., movies, and popular songs feed millions of emotionally starved people. The excessive use of drugs and the need for external materialistic gratification, are other attempts to fill this emotional vacuum. The need for external authorities, of course, also is part of this syndrome of authoritarian emotional self-denial. Giving up spontaneity and individuality, results in a thwarting or restricting of life energies. As Fromm so aptly put it: "psychologically, the automaton, while being alive biologically, is dead emotionally and mentally."[99]

As such, modern humanity, living in the authoritarian order, is starved for life. Since the authoritarian cannot experience life in the sense of spontaneous activity, which adds a lot of magic to every action, s/he needs replacement for this loss through any sort of excitement or thrill: films, T.V. etc., all the while paying in terms of material exchange for something that is lost in themselves.

The authoritarian child in school, however, is seldom aware of these discrepancies and unknowingly conforms to anonymous authorities, and adopts a self that is not his or her own. If life loses its meaning because it is not lived in terms of individual needs and uniqueness, humans become desperate. "The despair of the human automaton is fertile soil for the political and economic purpose of fascist control."[100]

Now that we have seen how students are conditioned to the point where they no longer know how to question, we will turn to what is put into their heads. This immediately brings up the issues of direct and indirect political propaganda, ranging from the pledge of allegiance and the subject matter in textbooks, to the questions of who controls the schools, and what is taught in them.

The main aim of our present educational system seems to be attaining the highest percentage possible of graduates who have been admitted to college. Parents leave it up to the 'experts' to decide what material or textbooks should be taught. The 'experts' include a maze of School Boards, textbook publishers and teachers. Publishers primarily want to sell books, and books that may 'rock the boat' don't generally sell. School Boards and teachers are usually interested in subject material that is directed toward a 'career' or job, and thus the subsequent attitudes, skills and values needed to 'fit in.'

In general, there is an attitude which promotes material instilling patriotism, obedience, loyalty, duty, honor and discipline. As such, the application of political propaganda is widely spread throughout course material, affecting students' identification with role-models, values and attitudes. History is the one example chosen to elaborate upon because it is directly relevant to this study. Political propaganda in schools is not a new or recent phenomenon.

Political propaganda, especially in the subject of history, has been and is commonplace in all national-authoritarian controlled systems of education. For example, during the war years of 1939-1945, the history texts fluctuated and changed in conjunction with the various political maneuvers. First, the Russians were our worst enemies, with Stalin depicted as a brutal tyrant, which he surely was. Then, we became allied with Russia against Hitler, and suddenly the Russians were our friends, 'such a good-natured, simple and down to earth people.' Then a few years later, after the Second World War, the Cold War set in, and Russia once again became the evil force in the North-East.

The amount of political propaganda used in our schools is, indeed, extensive. The way in which patriotic propaganda is presented, such as the propaganda glorifying our military for having 'saved' the Jews, defeating Hitler and Japan, in order to save 'the free world,' is not objective or holistic. The fact that America did not attack Germany to save the Jews, any more than Russia did for the same reason, is not even considered. As such, whole portions of history are conveniently omitted. Most of America and the rest of the world did not know about the concentration camps until the defeat and invasion of Nazi Germany, and those who did know mostly turned their backs on the victims trying to flee persecution. This was so because the 'final solution' for the Jews and others in the Nazi empire did not happen until the last part of the war, after the fall of Stalingrad and Africa, and after the American entrance into the war. Nor do the history books even consider that America possibly went to war for her own gain.

The possibility that the powerful groups involved in the arms race and militaristic imperialism, could have instigated or allowed Pearl Harbor to happen, in a similar fashion to the way in which the sinking of the ship Lusitania, carrying munitions, in the First World War, had been used to convince the isolationist American public into supporting a declaration of war, is not even considered. Nor is it mentioned that America conveniently waited until the world powers were thoroughly weakened before making a quick entrance, stealing the show from everyone.

A realistic evaluation of the outcome of World War II is also avoided. The fact that America and Russia both wanted control of Germany; for whoever controlled Germany effectively ruled Europe, is not mentioned. Yet, the obvious outcome of the war, the literal division of Germany and Europe into Russian and American respective spheres of influence, or control, is presented as though it was the natural outcome of the war. Also omitted is the fact that in this process Germany lost some 1/3 of her traditional land from which over 12 million ethnic Germans were brutally expelled as refugees, and what was left was divided into East and West Germany. There is also no mention of the fact that concentration camps, although the worst and most notorious are the Nazi camps, were not peculiar to Nazi Germany alone in World War II. Indeed, Stalin murdered millions of people in his Gulag concentration camps.

In this process, students are trained to react to stereotypes. Nationalism and superiority are associated with the 'good guys,' while the 'bad guys' are the 'fascists' or 'communists,' with no efforts made to discuss the real sources of this need for conflict, or to present a holistic view of the issues at hand. In this way, we can see that atrocities against humanity in World War II were not only those of the losers. Such facts as the Russian slaughters and massive purges of ethnic cleansing throughout Eastern Europe, as well as the American bombings of Dresden and Hiroshima, if even mentioned at all, are made to appear as isolated accidents.

Furthermore, no mention is made of the fact that the Nuremburg Trials, which punished some of the Nazi officials for their role in these atrocities against humanity, failed to punish the Allied officials for their share of atrocities. The same applies to subsequent wars and atrocities, such as those in Korea and Vietnam in which our 'officials' were not tried and punished for their part in obeying 'the orders.'

To return to the general topic of education, the conditioning and self-negation typical of our schools, produces children who are often ready to get rid of their individual selves and the responsibility to their own power and freedom, either by submission to external authorities, or by a compulsive conforming to accepted patterns. By using methods of conditioning such as conformity, categorizing, labeling, intimidation, ridicule, drugging, brain-washing, subduing, regimenting, breaking and conquering, any vestiges of individuality and personal power are destroyed.

In a sense, we do not have to wait for science to create machine robots, for our educational system is a mass assembly line of robots in the making, creating people who are regimented, stiff, rigid, conditioned and controlled. It is time to ask ourselves what the real purpose of education is? Is it a sharing, with others of all ages, of that which human evolution and experience has learned about what has helped people learn to be happy, secure within themselves and with others? Or is it an institution to train new workers and consumers, obedient and regimented automatons of an authoritarian machine-society?

In our lifetime we have seen the orientation of schools and colleges change from liberal arts or the holistic study of human knowledge, to a frantic competition to gain technological expertise which provides greater financial rewards in this age of science. Indeed, this tendency cannot go unnoticed and will, therefore, be expanded upon in the section on medicine and psychiatry, followed by a part on science and technology in general. The specific examples of medicine and psychiatry, will help to demonstrate the extent to which technological expertise and financial rewards have influenced our institutions. Medicine and psychiatry also are closely related to the central problem of education, namely, the use of institutions as systems of social conditioning and control.

MEDICINE

In the section on Institutionalism and Professionalism, we saw how there was a general tendency in our society to overemphasize the importance of both the experts and their institutions. In our zeal for developing institutions, their purpose has often changed from teaching personal order and growth to that of merely enforcing it. We also saw how running to the institutions and professionals, when faced with our own ineffectiveness or purposelessness is often the easy way out; an escape.

We have seen many examples of this increasingly dangerous reliance of people upon societal organizations for direction and the answers; from educational institutions, from organized religion, and from governmental institutions. People have felt increasingly less powerful in this process, seeking merely 'to fit in,' without ever questioning. In preferring to leave it all up to the institutions and professionals, in allowing someone else to be 'in charge,' people have forgotten that institutions and professionals can only help humans in their personal growth. To expect the source of personal growth, healing and power to be in the institutions or professionals, outside of ourselves, is an illusion and a form of escapism.

Although all institutions portray these same tendencies to varying degrees, the institution of medicine serves as an excellent example of how this over reliance upon institutions and professionals has come about.

The famous physician Paracelsus, born in a Swiss village in the year 1490, is greatly admired in the medical world for his research in medicine, especially in pharmacology. Paracelsus was also a great humanist and holistic healer. He claimed that a good doctor must recognize that nature is the ultimate physician, since holistically even a 'healer' is part of nature. Indeed, this strongly contradicts the prevalent conceptions of healing and health in which the conquering and control of nature, is applied to the area of medicine and healing as well. How can we be so arrogant as to want to control or conquer some thing as perfect and harmonious as nature? It may well be this need to 'control' our environment, including nature and humans, that is the source of a lot of human disease.

Paracelsus stated that a true healer would never consider financial advantages to be derived from his/her profession. Furthermore, he wrote that the mastery of the art of healing comes from experience and not from books, degrees or titles. Paracelsus achieved many remarkable cures, and was, in consequence, loved by his patients and hated by the authorities. He exposed the pomposity of the doctors of his day in very pungent words and as a result, lost his position in Basel. He was a lover of the people, speaking in their language, in German, rather than Latin, which then, as today, is used when speaking in medical terms. His writings demonstrate his immense knowledge of pharmacology, Alchemy, of homeopathic technique, of astrology and occultism. He was an ardent humanist, in personal contact with such great humanists as Erasmus of Rotterdam and Sir Thomas Moore.

Paracelsus' writings also show that he was aware of the more subtle levels of the human body, referring to the vital force, aura, and spirit, as important factors involved in the healing process. He believed in the individual power of humans to heal themselves and taught that will, love and imagination were magical powers possessed by every human being, which gave humans the power to create all that they are, including their physical and mental health. He also taught the ancient principle that the human is a microcosm, reflecting within oneself the universe, or the macrocosm, of which the human is but a small part. He believed in the age old concept that if humans understood themselves, they would understand the things of their inner world, that each human potentially had all the wisdom and power of the universe. Does Paracelsus sound like a typical physician of today?

Many of these concepts of healing have been lost in the maze of modern medicine, and its attempts to conquer and control illness. The American Medical Association is a huge political and economic organization, that has repeatedly shown that it is primarily interested in maintaining its position of power. As the 'official' organization of doctors it enjoys the profitable position of literally monopolizing the entire field of medicine. The social power of the title 'doctor' alone is augmented by the A.M.A.'s development of one of the most expensive and influential special interest group lobbies in the U.S. Congress. This political force has most effectively blocked any legislation not in their own interests. Furthermore, there exists an elaborate inter-relationship between hospitals, pharmacies, nursing homes, laboratories, and the pharmaceutical industry in which doctors play an important and profitable role.

At the same time there is a drastic shortage of doctors in America, which is hardly coincidental, but rather due to deliberate, yet subtly effective manipulation by the A.M.A.. Scarcity, of course, increases each doctor's market value and profit. This 'shortage' by its very nature, also increases the importance and power of doctors. As a result, our doctors have become an excellent example of professional elitism. It has now come to the point that doctors demand the right to control our bodies, seldom bothering to listen to patients or explain in understandable language what they are doing or why they are doing it. Forced sterilization of minority women, as well as the unquestioned use of drugs, and surgery, are only a few examples of this attitude.

Our hospitals are becoming monstrous technological machines that are rapidly creating a mechanistic-mystical view of healing and health. Scientific drugs, chemicals and technology are being seen more and more as the magical cure-all for human suffering. Although, drugs, for example, are seen as dangerous in the 'eyes of the law,' the pharmaceutical industries and doctors, continue to produce and dispense drugs at a rate that far exceeds any rational or even 'legal' need for them.

The specialized physician of today knows all about one area, but has little awareness of the sum-total of what s/he is actually doing. Medicine, for the most part, is no longer humanistic or holistic. Intrinsic to holistic medicine is that the parts of the whole of medicine or human health, can only be viewed in the perspective of their part in the whole. One particular part viewed by itself, can easily be misleading. As such, there are many parts and levels involved in the art of healing.

In the present system, the importance of the individual and his/her experience in the process of being healed or becoming whole has been lost to a large extent. Indeed, many people are getting tired of these mystifying doctors who always seem to have something up their sleeves, and being annoyed at anyone asking what it might be! The fact is that individuals do very much create their own physical condition through their thoughts, feelings and actions, just as medical research is presently 'discovering' the psychosomatic origin of so many disorders. One would think that the medical profession would then support people to get to the source of why they are ill, and help to teach them how to learn to be their own doctors. Yet, doctors are much more interested in treating the symptoms, by cutting out the illness or by blurring it with drugs, especially since there is much more profit in drugs and surgery.

Nonetheless, even after the illness has been cut out or drugged into oblivion, its origin is still there, in the psyche and thinking patterns of the individual. It is the individual person who, in the end, must learn how to heal himself/herself. Our medical organizations must learn to incorporate life-supporting and self-supporting attitudes, concepts and programs, that will assist and encourage people to take power within themselves in order to be whole. This will then demystify medicine and doctors. The more we do this, the less we will need to rely exclusively on institutions and professionals for our well-being.

This does not mean to infer that medical doctors are not needed. Quite on the contrary, holistic and humanistic healers or 'doctors' can be a great service to humanity in this process. A humanistic type of contact and service to people, can help return a sense of human proportions to the overwhelming and sterile atmosphere of present medical institutions. Our doctors need to become healers again, as they used to be. We need General Practitioners who practice humanistic and holistic medicine; who are able to incorporate all the parts of the whole of healing, including the psychological, spiritual and political dimensions of the patient. The ability to see personal growth in view of all the parts of the self, enables a healer to evaluate patients' conditions in terms of what they can do to become whole again.

New wonders in medical science and technology need to be brought into balance and harmony with the rest of the art of healing. There are many new and ancient disciplines of healing that incorporate the psychological, political and spiritual levels along with the scientific and technological. Many of these arts of healing are now being founded, revived and/or expanded, much to the dismay and wrath of the A.M.A. In spite of extensive research and development, alternative disciplines from Postural Integration to Reichian Therapy, have for the most part not been recognized or accepted by the American Medical Association or science. However, facts do not have to be 'scientifically proven' or accepted in order to be true. The earth rotated around the sun long before Copernicus scientifically 'discovered' and 'proved' that it did so. Another excellent example is the ancient art of acupuncture, which having been disapproved of for so long by the A.M.A., was finally accepted after the people's acceptance of it was so widespread that they could no longer ignore it. The one condition of its being recognized, however, was that all practitioners needed a medical degree recognized by the A.M.A. This prerequisite conveniently excluded most of the Chinese acupuncturists, to the benefit of the A.M.A.

The fate of Dr. Wilhelm Reich who helped to inspire many of these relatively new therapies, is indicative of how threatening these theories and methods are to the authoritarian structure. Wilhelm Reich was forced to flee Nazi Germany, only to be imprisoned, and die in a U.S. Federal Penal Institute for his views and work, a fact which in itself says something about the nature of fascism, and where it can be found. In addition to his imprisonment, the court ordered a book burning of over six tons of his publications, one of the most notable examples of American censorship.

In fairness, it must be noted that there are also a large number of medical doctors who are presently trying to create a more people-oriented and community centered application of medicine.

PSYCHIATRY

The psychiatric branch of medicine is also of interest to this study, especially since it can easily be used as a means of social control. In fact, psychiatry as we know it today, is notorious for its accommodation of the power relations of the society in which it functions. As such, psychiatry is often not an art of healing, but an oppressive force of social control. This is true of America, as well as the Soviet Union and most other powers.

Intrinsic to the practice of psychiatry is the belief that some behavior is 'normal', or 'sane', while others are 'abnormal' and 'insane'. Present exposure of what has been done under the name of treating insanity, is enough to make one extremely cautious of the entire area. Since insanity is presently loosely defined as the inability to deal with reality, the obvious question is whose reality is the standard, and the answer is frightening, to say the least. There are those of us who strongly question this authoritarian habit of defining and attempting to control 'what' is real and 'who' is real. It would do us well to start from the premise that we are all at least insane, at least to some extent, and that no one has an unwarranted right to set limits on anyone's reality.

In our society, a 'normal' or healthy person is stereotypically seen as a person who can fulfill the social role s/he is supposed to take. Psychiatry, as Eric Fromm notes, has largely made itself an instrument of the manipulation of personality: "many psychiatrists, including psychoanalysts, have painted the picture of a 'normal' personality which is never too sad, too angry, or too excited. They use words like infantile or neurotic to denounce traits or types of personalities that do not conform with the conventional pattern of a 'normal' individual." [101]

However, the person who is normal in terms of being well adapted, is often less healthy than the neurotic person in terms of human values. Often s/he is well adapted only at the expense of having given up his/her self, in order to fit the role s/he is expected to be. Very often any semblance of genuine individuality and spontaneity are lost in this identification with role-models.

136

On the other hand, the 'neurotic' person is often the person who will not compromise, and who refuses to surrender completely in this battle for his/her self. Indeed, s/he is not successful in terms of society, and may well be a victim of brutalization, yet from the standpoint of human values, s/he is less crippled than the 'normal' person who has lost his/her individuality and spontaneity altogether. [102]

The mental illness system, in its attempt to influence and mold people's personalities, can easily be restrictive and destructive to individual sensuous, emotional and intellectual expansion. The mental illness system supports and is supported by racism, sexism, authoritarianism, classism, ageism and capitalism. Therapists attempt to avoid political issues altogether, but what the therapists end up strengthening are those characteristics which most support the status quo, and therefore, they are actually functioning as highly political tools.

By undergoing 'successful' therapy, a person who might have been angry and therefore might have confronted the status quo is made to feel comfortable or complacent within it.[103] Psychiatry trains patients to look to the external society created roles in order to find themselves, instead of within themselves. Psychiatry trains people to distrust and hide their feelings and perceptions. Patients are taught to believe that they are 'sick' and 'inferior' to other people.

Mental institutions function like prisons and the threat of psychiatric imprisonment affects everyone. As such, psychiatry is a blatant form of social control. Therapy techniques read like a series of torture from some dungeon chamber: lobotomy, electroshock, chemicals, drugs, strait- jackets, chains and cells. This 'treatment' has now reached the point where electric 'brain pacemakers' are implanted in the skulls of patients.[104] As reported by Dr. Robert G. Heath of Tulane University, these pacemakers send tiny electrical currents into areas of the brain associated with pleasurable feelings, stimulating a so-called 'pleasure circuit' which produces 'instant-joy.'

Overlooked in this treatment, however, is the fact that any drug, machine or therapy that makes a person feel better, and does not change the objective conditions which created the 'bad feelings' or 'illness', lessons and often eliminates the person's motivation to confront and challenge the oppressive situation inside and/or outside of the self, which originally caused the problem. Inherent in this type of therapy, is a romantic escapism into mechanistic mysticism in which the individual loses personal power. Instead of becoming more whole, the psyche is drained and the person is therefore easily controllable. Furthermore, psychosurgery, drugs, shock and other treatments cut people off from their feelings and actively damage their minds.

In conjunction with its social control function, the mental illness system fosters sexism. The people with the most power in the mental illness system, as in other systems, are white men. Women are socialized into traditionally oppressive roles as servants and sex objects for men. Men are equally socialized in the traditionally oppressive roles of the dominating, unemotional, and aggressive providers.

At the same time, the mental illness system grossly coerces and oppresses lesbians and gay men. Other types of sexuality that are not conducive to the nuclear or patriarchal family (non-monogamy, bisexuality, and celibacy) are very conveniently seen as sick.

Old people are locked up in mental and other institutions in numbers disproportionate to their numbers in the population. Anyone who is not young, 'attractive' and/or not capable of working is more likely to be considered mentally ill. [105] Third World people are also locked up in disproportion to their numbers in the population. Women, African Americans, Mexicans, Native Americans, young people, old people, homosexuals, poor people, dissidents, the mentally challenged, and the 'rebellious' are the people who mostly suffer at the hands of these therapy institutions. It is here that the self- negating and life-negating forces of our society become a stark reality. The people who end up in these institutions are often the victims of psycho fascism, and are often a convenient supply of experimental fodder, where drugs, psycho-pharmacology and behavior modification techniques are used to forcefully recreate, alter and change human beings. In prisons and mental hospitals 'behavior modification' consist of psychosurgery, electroshock, massive drugging-especially Mellaril and Thorazine, adverse conditioning, sensory deprivation and more. Psycho-pharmacology and behavior modification have also found their way into our schools, where drugs such as Ritalin are freely given to so-called 'hyper active children'. Thorazine is also widely used in old age homes and institutions for the mentally challenged, as well as in juvenile reform schools.

America has more prisons and institutions for its misfits per population than any other nation. Today, for example, there are some 100,000 children imprisoned in the U.S., most having been put there for 'disobedience', for running away, for being 'ungovernable', or 'emotionally disturbed.' These prisons, called detention centers, reform schools and training schools are both oppressive and destructive to any vestiges of human indiduality.[106] They are also convenient dumping grounds for the mentally ill, where they receive little help or support. By creating institutions for anyone who does not fit the standards of what is considered 'normal', the reality of human variety is taken from us, and in its place is imposed a super-human standard of uniformity. This does not mean to imply that there are not those who could gain from a personalized institutionalization. Rather, the point is that there has been an over-emphasis upon the need for and function of such institutions .

The courts are now, as they have always been, in league with organized psychiatry in denying psychiatric inmates their human rights. The courts use 'contempt' of power if openly confronted, which puts a powerful political tool in the hands of psychiatry. The promotion of psychiatry and its therapies are supported by the corporations, the military, prisons and schools, all of which use psychiatric therapy in much the same way as in the mental illness system.

Indeed, the mystification of 'therapy' has become so wide spread and accepted in our society that its meaning has been lost. Therapy is essentially a human activity which has been preempted and monopolized by a professional elite, and sold as a commodity on the market.[107] As such, psychiatry has by in large become an industry, a machine and a system that is dehumanizing and not holistic.

Nonetheless, people involved in therapy, or interrelating with the purpose of helping people become healthy and happy, have two paths they can chose to follow. The first is the traditional method in which the individual is treated as if he/she is "sick" and "unhealthy," whereas society in general is seen as 'healthy'. Such a therapist tries to patch up the 'patient' to help him/her cope with the situation as it exists. This therapist is avoiding the central issues of why imbalance has developed in the patient in the first place.

The other type of therapist would realize that our society and its institutions mold and create one's patients, while, at the same time they teach people not to look within themselves for the answers. In realizing this, the therapist would immediately become a reformer as well, for the logical goal would then be to teach people to take power and responsibility for themselves, thus, helping to changing the whole phenomenon of human reality, including society and its institutions. This kind of therapy would help people to realize that only if we allow ourselves to be convinced that there is only one prefabricated version of reality can we fall prey to it, or be threatened by the ultimate psychiatric control: the verdict of 'insanity'.

This new type of therapy, which many alternative therapists are beginning to use, would by its very nature move away from the mechanistic-mystical view of healing. In this process the present use of technology as an agent of control, such as the indiscriminate use of drugs, brain pacemakers, electroshock treatments, psycho-surgery, etc. will need to be re-examined and much of it discarded. As an example, some state governments have recently begun to realize the past error of over-emphasizing gigantic, centralized and depersonalized therapy institutions. Instead they are embarking on programs of de-institutionalization with an emphasis upon community-based and operated facilities, which aim at integrating those who have been long hidden away back into society.

SCIENCE AND TECHNOLOGY

The original incentive for the development of technology was the desire to free humans from the burden of tiresome, mundane and time-consuming labor. Although science and technology have contributed greatly to the evolution of humanity, we have recently become aware that in many ways the freedom promised appears to be vanishing. Instead of improving and supporting human personal growth and happiness, it more often appears to be only strengthening the centralized control and authority of the power structure. Rather than appealing to human integrity, and supporting a meaningful environment within human proportions, it more often appears to be instilling fear, alienation, and a sense of powerlessness among the masses of people.

Although the field of science and technology is perhaps one of the most difficult for the average person to fathom, the growing concern over the quality of human life we view around us every day, is prompting more and more of us to confront the 'experts' on their grand schemes. Our long conditioned, supreme faith in science, along with the resulting mechanistic-mystical view of life is faltering. Our age old belief that, in some mysterious way, technology alone will somehow 'save' us, that it is our only hope and future, is being questioned. The old slogan "Better living through Chemistry' now appears to have been only a euphemism for more plastic. Technology itself is not the problem, and may well be central to solving our problems, but it's the type of technology and how we use it, that will make all the difference.

The more positive outgrowth of this disillusionment is symbolized by the new term 'appropriate technology'. This term carries great political implications, for implicit to its meaning is the radical concept that the people must share in making the decision, of whether or not a specific technology is appropriate in the larger context of the quality of human life. The ramifications of this change in public attitude are profound, for the results of this new experience of challenging the 'experts' has produced a new revelation: the figures posing behind the mystical shield of scientific expertise are most often not even the scientists themselves. Instead, they are the same economic vested interest groups whose authoritarian manipulation we have continuously encountered. The example of nuclear verses solar energy development is most illustrative of this situation.

> "The sun is the source of life on this planet. It seems almost perverse to talk of a thing of such infinite beauty in political terms. But there is, in fact, something subversive about the sun. It's free. It lasts too long. It falls on everyone equally. There's no way -yet -to monopolize it or dole it out to customers. And if there's a single reason why solar energy isn't our chief power supply today, that's it. The barriers are political, not technological."[108]

Although the technology necessary for large scale harnessing of the sun's rays for human lighting, heating and cooling needs has been proven and available for decades, and although its development has been continually proposed by governmental and academic studies, in the late 1950's the U.S. Government embarked on the 'Atoms for Peace' program. This decision to allocate tens of billions to nuclear energy research and development, despite the untold technical and legal difficulties such as the radioactive waste disposal problem unsolved to this day, makes complete sense only if seen within the political context in which it was made. Despite all its problems, nuclear energy has one tremendous 'advantage': it is a monopoly commodity in the best capitalistic sense of the word. Not only do atomic reactors require tremendous investments of capital to build, their operation can only be mastered by a technological elite, they require large maintenance costs, and they represent the epitome of centralized control.[109]

The actual nature of this 'advantage' can only be understood through another piece to the political power puzzle: the nature of the privately owned monopolies called 'public' utilities, which would become the heirs to this public appropriation of many billions of dollars. By law, a utility's profit is solely based upon a fixed return from its investment. It very simply can only increase its total revenue by spending more money; the more it spends, the more it makes. Hence, the prime social 'advantage' of nuclear energy is that it represents a profit bonanza for the utilities. As one of the most powerfully persuasive lobbies in Congress, and backed by the equally powerful oil lobby, it would surely be an understatement to say that the utilities interests were influential in the Government's decision to go with nuclear rather than solar energy.

In contrast, the development of solar energy represents the antithesis in social advantage. Not only does it require an initial minuscule capital investment, and little maintenance, it is such a relatively simple technology that even non-scientists can implement it. Even more threatening to the utility interests is the fact that solar power's most practical application is at the sub-community, if not individual dwelling unit level. Once installed, the family can even sell surplus power to the utility!

That, in a nut-shell, is the problem, for as Wasserman aptly notes, "The major energy corporations now live in terror of a solar economy."[110]The availability of a source of power which even the smallest community could implement on its own would destroy multinational energy investments. Since at least $200 billion is now tied up in nuclear investments alone, not including fossil fuel investments by utility and oil companies, many of the wealthiest vested interests stand to lose a great deal of wealth and power if solar or wind energy should be allowed to compete.

Despite the many millions which have been spent to convince the public that solar energy is not 'realistic', and that nuclear energy is not only 'safe' but somehow directly linked to America's mystical destiny, it appears that solar energy is an idea so ripe that nothing can hold it back. Although, even a minimal government investment in solar research would speed its development tremendously, small alternative companies have, nonetheless, formed to produce solar systems for home application and the cost continues to drop. Now that solar energy can no longer be ignored, even the big utilities are getting into the act by creating a media image that they are at the vanguard of solar research. Aside from buying and burying patent rights, their sole focus is upon promoting centralized solar applications so that they can still control the energy supply. Even though such mammoth applications would be much less energy-efficient than individually owned and operated units on every roof-top, the utilities have nevertheless, received the majority of governmental research funding to date, in order to develop centralized applications.

This example clearly demonstrates the danger of a complacent public, all too eager to avoid any responsibility to personally confront problems directly effecting their lives and lifestyles. To unquestioningly rely upon an external authority's determination of 'appropriate' very often leads to the policies contrary to the public's best interests.

The military establishment's utilization of science is, of course, a most blatant example of the use of technology to further authoritarian control. Although the general topic has been covered under the heading of Militarism, the neutron bomb deserves to be mentioned. It is perhaps a tribute to the present state of the mass consciousness, when the Government feels that it can sell the public the need for this new weapon upon the justification that it is 'more humane' in that it kills people without destroying property.

Equally important as these blatant uses of technology as vehicles of authoritarian control are the more subtle applications. The technological innovation of television, for example, demonstrates again how people have abdicated their power over its application and content. It also very clearly demonstrates how profoundly people can be affected by technology on a subtle level. Since corporate America directly controls the video message

144

through their commercial sponsorship, it is little wonder that the primary message is that of consumerism.

Although television itself represents the potential of being used as a tremendous societal asset, this very asset can become a liability when the 'appropriateness' of the message is left to others to decide. The possibilities of public education and personal growth, and development, presented through television's potential to broaden the individual's reality has been largely sacrificed to the interests of profit and sensationalism. Not only can TV very effectively implant values, beliefs, desires and fears in the viewer without his/her conscious awareness of the process, it can also implant an entire 'Weltanschauung'. When passively watching TV replaces the individual's own process of active relatedness, as it has for so many people, then it becomes a most pervasive force for the molding of the person's conception of reality itself.[111] In terms of the authoritarian threat of centralized control and standardization, television presents perhaps the ultimate weapon: The TV Reality, consciously manufactured and controlled by a very select few, the very antithesis of what television could be.

In terms of the individual, television can serve as a persuasive force against the need for any personal and spontaneous relatedness, an easy way out for those who are unwilling to experience their own lives in terms of their actual situation. It can become merely an external diversion for the actual boredom and alienation of the individual's life, replacing the need for personal creativity and uniqueness.

THE WORK ETHIC

In our society the joint conditioning of the patriarchal family and religion, have had a profound effect upon the individuals very conception of the word 'work'. As we saw in the introductory comparison of the matriarchal and patriarchal world views, the matriarchal support of an inherently self-defined conception of happiness and success, became one of an imposed and singularly material definition under patriarchy. The term individual became equated with 'production unit', and personal growth and development took on the connotation of 'marketable skills'.

The influence of the Protestant Reformation and its 'work ethic' of striving and frantic activity only intensified the conflict. When material success became interpreted as a sign of God's grace, and material failure a sign of damnation, the internalized compulsion for unceasing work produced individuals who were their own slave masters.

Thus, we can see how the concept of 'work' became solely an externally imposed concept of 'what one has to do to pay the bills'. Once 'work' had become separated from any personally defined sense of individual growth and fulfillment, work became the substitute for it. Despite the resulting self-alienation, personal 'success' became merely a cog-like efficiency in the wheel of economics. Rather than 'losing' contact with one's individual purposefulness, it would be more accurate to say that the authoritarian individual never developed one in the first place.

As we have constantly seen, each step in the loss of self-power is registered as a gain for someone else. The economic interest groups, symbolized by the employer, greatly benefit by holding the power to define what is to be considered socially 'productive' for the rest of society. If work in our society was supported as necessarily connected with personal growth for the good of each individual, then vast segments of our economy would have to be re-evaluated and made socially meaningful, or economically attractive if anyone would be expected to perform those tasks.

This is, however, not part of the definition of socially 'productive' provided to us by a capitalist economy. Indeed, as societies became more 'advanced', the problem is conveniently solved through the prerogative of wealth and power exploitation of another people. As is the case with every industrialized nation around the world, another people are invariably found who are desperate enough to be forced to do the dirty work. If they aren't desperate enough, there are many novel ways to make an entire country most desperate. Switzerland imports 'guest laborers' to do the considerable work which the natives find beneath them, workers who are treated distinctly in keeping with their last-class status. In England the Irish have long served this purpose, explaining the need for their continued domination. In America, the obvious example of the African slaves is continued today in the treatment of the Mexican farm workers in the Southwest.

In the previous section on The Reformation, we saw how the rise of industrialization and monopolistic control of capital, caused other crucial changes in the human conception of 'work' in relation to the individual. With the introduction of hourly wages, time increasingly became a supreme value with even minutes becoming important. The ideas of 'efficiency' and 'productivity' assumed new roles of importance which even surpassed quality and the worker's skill at the craft. With everyone emerging as a potential competitor, people became isolated and threatened. As the old way of personally defining and controlling one's livelihood began to die away, so did job security and a great deal of the personal fulfillment. The concept of work became more and more the role of a servant to the economic machine and those who controlled it. Moreover, anyone who resisted became among the damned, the lazy or the social parasites.

Thus, a very small group controlling the economic system can intimidate the population by means of the pay check, bribing and co-opting the workers by the illusion of material rewards held out like a carrot on a stick. In America today, however, there is a large working class which actually includes the middle class, and it is alive but not so well. These people are hardly able to enjoy the promised 'good life' if they have to work up to 60 hours a week just to pay for it. For most, the American Dream is something they only see on television. Little time or money is left over for the pursuit of other human aspirations, and their upward mobility is largely a cruel myth. What little material rewards they do receive are most often on credit, and are but mere crumbs.

In addition, governmental planned unemployment increases job insecurity, raking havoc with unionization, and result in making people feel grateful for any job at all.

In this materialistic society, people not only sell commodities, they also sell themselves and feel themselves to be a commodity. [112] Thus, an individual's personal self-identity tends to become less based upon their internal knowledge of themselves, than on a job based on competitive popularity in the labor market. People, therefore, adopt socially created roles, images and lifestyles in order to be 'successful'. What is lacking in terms of personal happiness and fulfillment is often compensated for through external validation. Material reward is perhaps the most persuasive compensation, the purpose for the long hours of alienating employment, and the main component of the American Dream.

ADVERTISING

Advertising can play a constructive role in society through the mass communication of material commodities and services, which individuals might seek to utilize for the enrichment of their lives. Within this context, advertising can contribute to a more informed public, one which is better able to discern the range of their options. These societal advantages, however, can be greatly outweighed when the role of advertising changes to primarily that of the manipulation of the consumer. Once the genuinely self-conceived needs of the consumers have been provided for, however, there is no longer a market; a situation which capitalism finds very hard to accept. It is the producer, rather than the consumer, who benefits when advertising becomes a force which subtly implants new needs and desires within the consciousness of the consumer; needs which are manufactured just as literally as the commodities themselves.

Through our study this far, it should be quite evident that the typical consumer is in a very vulnerable position, one which Corporate America has not failed to exploit down to the smallest detail. Through the pervasive influence of the patriarchal family, church and state, the individual has been largely stripped of any internal sense of confidence, personal identity, purposefulness or direction in life, and is instead primarily dependent upon external authority. As such, the individual is so self-alienated that s/he is tremendously susceptible to external manipulation, no matter how irrational the authority may actually be. In this internal vacuum, people can become so desperate that they can easily be prompted to frantically attempt to support an external substitute for the meaningfulness so sorely missing inside. It is this need to find compensation for the inner desolation which is constantly reinforced, and played upon by advertising. Since it is the sole goal of the advertiser to sell its merchandise, it is hardly coincidental that we live in a society founded and built upon the illusive compensation of material rewards.

The average American sees many hundreds of advertisements a day, all of which effect him/her subconsciously, if not consciously. Most modern advertising does not appeal to reason, but to emotion. As Fromm notes, "like any other form of hypnotic suggestion, it tries to impress its objects emotionally and then make them submit intellectually."[113] Thus, the consumer is influenced in countless ways, for the emotional weaknesses of the authoritarian individual are many. The repetition of the same slogan over and over, or the image of an authoritarian figure such as a football star who uses a certain credit card, or buys only a certain brand of beer, are only a few of the many subliminal methods of advertising which are essentially irrational in that they have nothing to do with the qualities of the products. Instead, they merely serve to blur and destroy the critical capacities of the customer, like a strong drug or outright hypnosis. Such blatant attempts at emotional manipulation could not be effective if the majority of the public were not so emotionally starved.

The constant promotion of images and role-models has a very strong subconscious effect. The presentation of what appear to be happy and successful individuals wearing certain clothes, and acting in a deliberately pre-defined manner, create the impression that if

149

the consumers would only purchase these clothes and act this way, then they too will belong to that mystically special group and finally gain 'happiness'. These external replacements, however, cannot be purchased without a price, and a steep one at that. Not only do 'you get what you pay for', but job enslavement, in order to buy all this stuff, is very often the result. How many products have we all been convinced to buy in an unconscious attempt to buy back our self-esteem, and how much self-esteem have we all lost in trying to pay for them?

There is perhaps a product and a sales gimmick to cash in on every imaginable human weakness. The fear of death so prevalent in our culture is consciously manipulated into a marketable 'need' which affords life Insurance companies their tremendous wealth and power. As opposed to the matriarchal extended family, the patriarchal family structure breeds human groupings which are alienated from one another, and in which each family unit is totally dependant upon only one member, usually the father, to fulfill all material needs. This situation, as we have seen, produces a wife and children who are considered innately incapable of providing for their own needs. It should be remembered, however, that somehow people have existed for ages without this relatively recent 'necessity'. It is perhaps the ultimate in external validation to conceive that one is 'successful' in that one is worth $100,000 to his family upon death.

Although marketing has been known to utilize virtually anything possible to manipulate the potential customer, the tremendous sexual frustration of a patriarchal society is perhaps the most exploited of all. The entire cosmetic industry is integrally connected to bodily guilt. Make-up, deodorants and perfumes, for example, are promoted in such a way as to implant the feeling that our very bodies are somehow shameful, disgusting, ugly, dirty and smelly embarrassments which we must therefore pay to camouflage.

Despite commercial reinforcement of the sexual stereotypes and taboos of the patriarchal order, our denied sexual urges are most profitably sold back to us through the use of sexual gimmicks which attract attention and weaken the critical abilities of the customer. Sexuality sells, and it's little wonder. 'Attractive' and 'sexy' women and men are used to push everything from joining the Navy to buying cigarettes. Although commercial slogans such as "flick your Bic" and "did you get stroked this morning" (a shaver ad) carry most blatant phallic overtones, the advertisers themselves feign amazement at their appeal and insist that any sexual connotation is only coincidental. They are successful only because the populace is so generally sexually inhibited. Authoritarian individuals are so vulnerable to sexual suggestion because they are unable to actually experience their own sexual fantasies and desires in any active manner.

A related outgrowth of this manipulation is the distortion and perversion of the meaning of words through their commercial usage. Much of modern advertizing is a reflection of our general destruction of the precision of our language through our addiction to superlatives. Panty hose are not only marketed as being sexy, but as 'fantastic' and an 'extraordinary breakthrough' as well. Since words create, when they lose their meaning, they create meaninglessness. When panty hose become 'revolutionary', then you know that the revolution is over.

The language of a people is reflective of the consciousness of the people who must speak it. Just as we saw how the Nazi era altered the German language, changes in a language reflect changes in the people's consciousness as well. Indeed, the deliberate debasement of a language debases the collective consciousness. As much of the language becomes blurred, so does the ability to communicate with it, and thus comprehend what others are saying.

The area of political advertising is a relevant demonstration of the societal consequences of this debasement of people's critical capacities. Confronted with an awesome and needlessly mystified political process, most of today's voters are as alienated from the actual functioning of their government, as they are from the corporate empire for which they daily toil. It has often been stated that the electoral process has been irreversibly altered by the electronic media, particularly television. It could also be stated, that the personage who occupies the Oval Office at any given time has been literally sold to the public as effectively as the currently leading brand of aspirin.

It's hardly coincidental that an alarming number of Nixon's top staff were originally trained in their craft on Madison Avenue. At election time, political ads must indeed compete with products which solemnly pledge to magically remove the grimy build-up from the corners of the kitchen floor quick-as-a-wink-or-your-money-back. The serious discussion of any of the critical problems facing society, however, is avoided as meticulously as a carcinogenic side effect, for hard facts are not nearly as convenient as simplistic slogans. Even if appeals to base emotionalism should somehow fail, then factors which have absolutely nothing to do with the question at hand, can always be paraded around like scantily clad models until any rational discernment left in the public has been numbed. Study after study has shown that very few voters have any idea what they actually voted for, not to mention why.

V

THE CULMINATION: THE AMERICAN 'NEW RIGHT' MOVEMENT

N ow that we have taken a look at a great many of the individual parts of fascism in America and elsewhere, this chapter will attempt to holistically view the phenomenon. In doing so, we will see how the mass internalization of extreme authoritarianism creates a sense of 'need' which, unless effectively countered, must eventually become manifest in the external development of organized political fascism. Before moving to the presently blossoming 'New Right' movement in American politics, however, it is necessary to briefly bring together the personal attributes which characterize the individuals who are fueling the need for such a fascistic movement.

Throughout this book the subtle effectiveness of contemporary fascism has been repeatedly demonstrated. It has been discovered that authority does not need to take the form of a person or institution; external authority can also appear internally under the name of duty and/or conscience, a force which can rule the individual as firmly as, and perhaps even more effectively than, blatant external forms. Although a genuinely self-developed sense of conscientiousness can prove to be a great strength to the individual, quite frequently the contents of the orders issued by the conscience are not governed by the demands of the individual self, but instead by societal demands: the morals, norms, taboos, ethics and the resulting fear and guilt which have been implanted there through the social conditioning previously discussed.

This conditioning is so subtly pervasive that few are even aware that they possess the potential to develop a truly individualized sense of conscience. This can put the individual in a most unfortunate predicament, for the individual usually believes that the orders are his/her own. Instead of the individual's self-authority, however, an anonymous authority actually reigns.

Most people, of course, are not aware that they have only been duped into believing that they are free and powerful, that they actually make up their own minds. This situation is dangerous because when an external authority rules, it is clear that there are orders and who is giving them; thus, one can fight against such control. In anonymous authority, however, both command and commander have become invisible. [114]

The end result is an individual who believes that s/he is free and self-willed. Yet somehow this same individual, ends up supporting the same ideals, values and needs as the individual who is ruled outright by a master. Thus, there are two basic fascistic individuals: the one who is blatantly controlled by an external power; and the individual deluded into believing that s/he is self-willed, yet is actually just as controlled as the former.

The authoritarian individual loves those conditions in which a predefined and clear structure of 'good and bad' is dictated. Crisis and prosperity are not seen as politically manipulated phenomena, which might therefore be changed through human activity, but instead as necessary evils which are 'dealt' with through competition to 'get one's share' . There is always a 'higher' authority, outside of the self, towards which one must look for guidance. There is a strong conviction that life's conditions are determined by forces outside of one's self, that such forces are impossible to be rationally understood, and hence the only happiness lies in compromise and/or submission to these powers.

The authoritarian person worships the security of the past, from the Old Testament to Karl Marx. A spontaneous thought or action is outside the range of his/her emotional experience. Incapable of being fully aware and powerful in the present, such people tend to see everything from the perspective of what has been and what is said to have been. There is complete lack of faith in the ability of the self to create and 'be' whatever the self wills, desires and imagines, other than through mystical release.

We have also seen that the authoritarian person, or automaton, is in a condition of extreme desperation, whether consciously aware of it or not. The amount of destructiveness to be found in people is proportionate to the degree to which the expansiveness of growth has been curtailed and/or restricted. When the inner dynamics of life have been blocked, stopping all spontaneity, growth, and expression of our sensuous, emotional and intellectual capacities, we become desperate for a release. Such release very often manifests in the form of destruction.

There is virtually nothing that has not been used as a rationalization for this need to destroy; love, duty, conscience, patriotism, racism, save the children, save the family, and protect the honor of the nation, all have been, and are still being used as disguises and excuses to destroy others and/or oneself. All is seen in terms of 'good or bad,' 'powerful or weak', and hence the automaton desperately tries to identify with the 'powerful' and the 'good guys' . Lastly, we have perceived that not only will automatons do anything to avoid taking their own personal power and the responsibility for it, but they are also very gullible to anyone or anything that promises to fill that vacuum.

The automaton is alive and 'well', and not at all that uncommon. In fact, perhaps the great majority of people in our society have ceased to be themselves, and instead have adopted the personality and life style offered by cultural patterns created on

Madison Avenue. As such, they are exactly as everyone expects them to be. This mass illusion of individuality and personal freedom is most dangerous, for it blocks the removal of those conditions that created, and continue to create, that illusion.

We are programmed and manipulated to such a degree that self-alienation has resulted on a mass scale. This has caused the loss of self-knowledge and self-power, often without our knowing it, until, we have almost lost the memory that we were once quite different, and still could be. This is the energy source of destructiveness, and very fertile ground for the societal development of overt, political fascism. All that are needed now are the right 'issues', economic conditions, and 'leaders' to mold this existing alienation into a potent political force. We will now look at each one of these factors in analyzing the growing American 'New Right' movement, drawing parallels to the rise of fascism in pre-Nazi Germany whenever applicable.

THE ISSUES

The issues, of course, have always been there. It is merely a matter of exploiting them at the most appropriate time. When the general alienation of the masses is intense enough, it makes them not only easily susceptible, but to be almost searching for, fascistic 'solutions'. These 'solutions', however, seldom deal with the real or central problems at hand, but instead only blur them with emotional appeals to the people's sense of unfairness, hostility and fear, as well as distrust of those who are to blame. Those who are to blame for the problem end up as 'the enemy', a convenient scapegoat to relieve any personal responsibility for the situation.

Hitler's anti-Bolshevism blamed the Communists for street chaos and various other social problems in a way that is very similar to the fear of 'communism' in America today. Hitler's promise of 'law and order' and a 'moral clean-up' of the nation also sound familiar. This propaganda, as we have seen, appealed most to the Protestant youth groups and Bible circles which abounded in Germany at the time, much as the 'Jesus Movement' and various extreme fundamentalist Protestant movements flourish in America today. In times of crisis an authoritarian state always accentuates the 'need' for law and order, morality, and the protection of the family, children and nation, for it knows well the root of its structural power. In the Nazi example, 'decadence', 'sexual filth' and 'corruption' were all societal threats imputed to 'the inferiors', whether they be aliens, Jews, communists or homosexuals.

In modern America, despite the dramatic decline of 'mainline' religions, there has been a marked revival of extreme fundamentalist Christian movements. As Rice University sociologist William Martin notes of the estimated 45.5 million 'born-again' evangelicals, they "have become the most active and vital aspect of American religion today."[115] With few exceptions, these movements are not only morally righteous, but rightist as well, creating a new, ultra-conservative political force based upon 'Christian principles'. Bill Bright's 'I Found It' campaign, for example, is an evangelical movement which is attempting to organize a nation wide, right-wing Christian force. Similar to the Moonies, the 'I Found It' people are ardently anti-communist, wanting 'to get America back on a sound military and economic basis'. Not coincidentally, Moon and Bright share many of the same backers, some of the most active U.S. supporters of the repressive Park regime.[116]

Any political campaign which espouses fundamentalist concepts of morality is both irrational and escapist. Quoting selected passages of the Bible to oppose women's equal rights, gay rights, abortion, adultery or divorce is a most dangerous projection of one's own irresponsibility onto others. Not only can the Bible be interpreted in many different ways by simply ignoring that which does not comply with some preconceived notion, but the whole process is irrational. If we literally followed the Old Testament, we'd be committing sins by eating rabbit, lobster, clams, shrimp, oysters, rare steak; by cutting beards (all in Leviticus); or by wearing wool and linen at the same time (Deuteronomy). Not too long ago devout Christians were supporting slavery and the complete subservience of women because it was 'endorsed' by St. Paul.

Again, we find the same kind of slogans used in these moral campaigns as in pre-Nazi Germany: dangers to the sanctity of the family, religion, nation and God . Part of the Nazi attack on the very extensive German counterculture consisted of the out-right condemnation and eventual extermination of many thousands of homosexuals. Public crusades against 'decadence', especially prostitution and homosexuality, complete with comparisons of the Fall of Rome, and Sodom and Gomorrah, were very common just before and during the rise of the Nazi regime in Germany. These are merely typical attempts of the authoritarian automatons to vent their own sexual frustration and insecurity, to feel 'normal' and therefore 'better' than someone else, and at the same time procure a convenient scapegoat for all the world's problems.

Similar arguments are being used today, even in the halls of congress, in the anti-abortion, anti-ERA, and racial discrimination issues. To quote the Bible as proof for the subservience of women to men, of all other races to whites, is to take the Bible out of its context. The Bible was written in another age, for a people who's material needs and culture were radically different than ours today. If the Bible opposes abortion on the grounds of the "sanctity of human life', than how can the same people support the death penalty so fervently, not to mention the military or the neutron bomb? In blowing up the issues into emotionally charged good/bad morality campaigns, all sight of holism is lost. The hypocrisy of such tactics, as well as the benefit to those who stand to lose control if people should figure out what really oppresses them, are self-evident.

The anti-ERA campaign to keep women in the home, family bound, God-fearing, and obedient to their man, is a tactic that was also successfully used by the Nazis, as we saw earlier in the chapter on Nazi development in Germany. The Nazis also opposed abortion, promoting instead the role of women as vessels of God and the State, loosely translatable as baby machines. How this kind of thinking develops, is reflected in the following present day example. Dorothy Waldvogel, a 46 year old mother in Bensenville,

Illinois, U.S.A., aptly expresses the 1977 attitudes of the American 'New Right" constituency.

> "There was abortion, and then the homosexual movement was getting so big. And then Illinois was the key state for the E.R.A. You know something is wrong, but you need someone to tell you how to get involved. So some of the girls down at the church made up a list of state legislators. I sat down and wrote 65 letters, all about the importance of the family, and how male and female are different. I mean, how can a law make males and females the same? To me, the E.R.A. is an attack on our system of life - call it tradition - the way God intended it to be." [117]

For Dorothy Waldvogel, as for many women and men of what is so often written off as simply 'Middle America', the perception that "something is wrong" is becoming inescapable. The family appears to be the best available rock in a time of turbulent and contradicting social issues, while they are searching for someone to tell them how to 'get involved.'

Behind the New Right vanguard of the 'pro-family' front are scores of battles which may seem separate, yet basically appeal to the same alienated constituency. Sooner or later, as Andrew Kopkind notes in the New Times magazine, pro-family activists find themselves also as pro: death penalty, nuclear power, local police, F.B.I., C.I.A., defense budget, Panama Canal, and public prayer. They are also more than likely to be anti: busing, welfare, gun control, amnesty, marijuana, gay liberation, day-care centers, religious ecumenism, car pools, the 55 mph speed limit, public employee unions, affirmative action, communes, pornography, sex education, abortion, and the Environmental Protection Agency.[118]

The busing issue is an example of emotional manipulation of an extreme sort, in that it plays upon racist fears and prejudices. It is handled in an irrational manner, only blurring the central problems which are never dealt with. The real issue is not the busing of students from here to there, but the more incriminating fact that there are no decent schools, housing or employment for the people whose children are being used as pawns in the larger social conflict. To move disadvantaged children from one poor school to another poor one, while the wealthy white suburbs are conveniently ignored, creates so much understandable hostility that any 'theoretical' advantages are more than offset.

The patriotic and nationalistic issue of the Panama Canal, was an issue mined for its emotional appeal to a nationalistic sovereignty that has 'destined' America to selflessly protect the interests of the entire hemisphere, although the extreme right slogan 'There is no Panama Canal, only an American Canal in Panama' surprisingly expresses the real motive. Patriotic causes that play on national 'enemies' are classical fascist tools, and after this one there is sure to be another. The authoritarian loves to refer to the 'days when America never lost anything', and places critical importance on keeping ahead in the arms race, for these are typical external projections and replacements for individual weakness and insecurity.

The recent revival of the death penalty all across the country is but the latest in the 'law and order' agenda, the only casualty thus far being the defeat of Senate Bill One, at least for now. Despite the psychologically proven irrationality of the death penalty's deterrence of crime, it is merely a reflection of the collective fear, restriction, self-negation and need for illusions of security that create the need for such a vengeance upon "bad" people. It is particularly reassuring to them that almost all of such executions are of the 'weak' and 'powerless' disadvantaged minorities whom they so despise for their differentness.

The growing demand for and actual increase in the numbers of police and special tactical squads are reminiscent of the rise of fascism in Germany. When it comes to the point that people who desire to demonstrate in public against their oppression must ask for a permit in order to be allowed to confront one of these anti-riot squads, then one can be sure that a major portion of our freedom under the law has been lost. The list could go on and on,

160

yet the critical connection to make is that each issue concerns the restriction of human self-determination, and that the coalition behind each includes those whose lack of any self-identity is threatened by those who take their own power.

THE ECONOMIC CONDITIONS

Although economic problems are very complex, and perhaps beyond the range of this book, they are nonetheless crucial to a political analysis and therefore, deserve close attention. The example of pre-Nazi Germany showed that the severe economic problems resulting from the loss of World War I, and thus, the loss of its 'empire', and the following successive depressions, were all decisive factors in the development of the German need for a more authoritarian state. Political agents who tend towards fascistic 'solutions' consistently take advantage of the populace's grave material fears in order to obtain more power, and are not above the actual creation of such economic 'crises'.

The defeat of the U.S. in Vietnam is highly symbolic of the inability of American imperialism to continue to exploit the entire world, for the many colonial revolutions, both direct and indirect, are causing the inevitable weakening of the global American economic empire. The growing internal economic problems of unemployment, inflation, the energy crisis, and the urban fiscal crisis, are merely the natural consequences of an economic empire which is no longer expanding. This serious threat to corporate American power, due to the growing loss of the traditionally cheap resources and captive markets for expensive manufactured goods, must eventually effect the economic security of all Americans, for our material wealth is based on it.

At present we are not feeling the full momentum of this economic change, as we still have one of the very highest standards of living on the planet, based upon the consumption by our 1/20th of the global population, of one third of the entire world's resources. This situation is bound to change, however, since even if American sheer militaristic force should be allowed to continue such exploitation, the unavoidable fact remains that these resources themselves have become severely depleted. In addition, the many revolutions and people's struggles throughout the empire are causing the wealthy capitalists to flee to America, a last safe frontier for the rich. Since these individuals are the most proficient in the exploitation of others, there is no reason to believe that they will not continue this practice in America.

The destruction of the Weimar Republic showed that in a time of economic panic, particularly if the only basis of individual security is in external materialism, the great middle classes are extremely susceptible to fascistic 'solutions', especially if the anti-fascistic forces are divided, weak, and unable to offer viable alternatives which address the very real fears of authoritarian individuals.

The American people today are becoming more and more panicky, as the economic situation continues to deteriorate. This process will surely become much more intense as the economic empire continues to slowly crumble. As this happens, social programs get cut, prices go up, real and manipulated shortages appear, and people find themselves competing more and more for fewer available jobs. When this happens, one minority traditionally gets pitted against another in a fight to 'get their share', and the thin veneer of constitutional, or 'human' rights becomes most apparent.

As Dorothy Waldvogel so aptly stated, the masses of middle class Americans are indeed coming to the inescapable awareness that there 'is something wrong', and therefore, we will now turn to the question of who can best 'tell them how to get involved' .

THE QUESTION OF LEADERSHIP

At present, there is no publicly identified leader of the 'New Right', a politically nebulous term, which is becoming closely identified with the coalescence of the alienated, authoritarian individuals we have been discussing around the issues just enumerated. The mere existence of the term, the 'New Right' however, demonstrates the increasing amount of organization taking place behind the scenes, including a most definite search for a powerful leader.

To put this into a political context, it is important to understand that historically the American 'two party system' has had the effect of moderating, if not stifling, the variety of organized political opinion. Since any political aspirant is thus required to slowly rise through one of the two very confining hierarchies, the main criteria is 'don't rock the boat if you want to get ahead'. As well as limiting 'radical' progress, this conformity has also limited extreme reactionary 'backslide' to an equal degree, by blocking most bids for power on the part of the more fascistic of the right-wing elements.

Officially leaderless, the more authoritarian-minded people have tended to be apolitical, supporting Democrats on 'pocket book' issues, and Republicans on the more 'law and order' issues, generally speaking. Both parties have been controlled by an intellectual elite with direct ties to the material elite, and as such, these political theoreticians have never felt comfortable with either the rationale nor economic demands of the reactionary right.

For that matter, neither party has been able to deal concretely with the very real issue of the alienation and frustration of the people in general, the established left as well as the right. When seriously confronted with the peoples' real problems, the 'liberals' tend to feel guilty and throw money at the problems, while the 'conservatives' look for any 'answer' that will not seriously incriminate 'free enterprise' .

In the past, most of these 'irrational' reactionaries were successfully purged from the Republican Party by the purer theorists, creating a situation in which no political outlet was allowed for the expression of the 'common people's' frustrations. This does not mean, however, that this group is small. To the contrary, there is an extremely large, though dormant, constituency of right-wing reactionaries who can easily be ignited. This was explicitly demonstrated by the large support George Wallace received in his 1968 primary campaign, actually carrying Michigan and Maryland.

There are now, however, many signs that this political force is being quietly organized around the entirely new banner of the 'New Right', and around issues that transcend the two parties and their inability to confront and deal with the issues relevant to this 'pro-family' front. The anti-ERA, anti-abortion, anti-gay liberation, and anti-busing movements, among others, are serving to catalyze the 'New Right' and its search for a charismatic leader.

This movement's two most public figures thus far have been Phyllis Schlafly and Anita Bryant. Bryant's 'Save our Children' campaign against the gay anti-discrimination ordinance in Dade County, Florida, brought her into almost every American living room as the champion of the moral fiber of the nuclear family. She pledged to take her campaign all across America.

Her campaign was basically a politicized fundamentalism over the 'human rights' of the majority over a scapegoat minority. Her overall political message, however, included anti: abortion, alcohol, adultery, 'fornication', cohabitation, and even nudity. She was taken most seriously by the public: the 1977 Gallop Poll lists her as America's third most admired woman.

Although Bryant's sincere, yet naive political awareness would not seem to make her a likely candidate for any role other than a media gimmick. Phyllis Schlafly, on the other hand, may well hold a better chance at assuming actual leadership capacity. As well as already showing considerable organizational talent, her anti-ERA crusade for woman's 'rights', husband, God and family notwithstanding, is a most effective issue to coalesce the New Right. It most deviously incorporates many of the most appealing issues, such as sex, big government, family, morality, lesbianism, God, etc. .

Schlafly's ferocious 'Eagle Forum' is the virtual voice of the national anti-ERA movement, successfully creating a 'counter-revolution' to the woman's liberation movement. Her success in this endeavor has reached the point that masses of women throughout the country have been convinced that their equality is in fact a loss of 'rights' . It is in this manner that the ERA has been defeated in every state where it has been at issue in the last two years, with the sole exception of Indiana.

Much more hidden behind the scenes, however, is an individual to whom the New Right owes much of its current ascendancy. Richard Viguerie, an arch-rightist political fund-raising and direct-mail specialist, is a very powerful force in this new movement, and is widely acknowledged as such. Alan Crawford describes him as the 'prime mover' behind the New Right in The Nation thusly:

> "Having amassed a small fortune in direct-mail fund rising, Viguerie now enjoys a position of leadership that he could never have attained within the G.O.P. He has become the prime mover behind what he likes to call the 'New Right', a loosely tied group of political action organizations created to compete with the traditional center of power on the American right. ... A virtuoso in the advertising medium that ranks third behind television and the newspapers, he maintains a staff of 250 non union employees in Falls Church, Virginia, to send out 50 million pieces of mail each year from 250 mailing lists that contain the names of 10 million Americans. Viguerie brings in at least $25 million a year for his growing list of clients; he raised $6 million from 1974 to 1976 for George Wallace. Other clients have included Citizens for Decent Literature, Conservative Books for Christian Leaders, the National Rifle Association, and No Amnesty for Deserters - names which reflect Viguerie's political concerns." [119]

The Watergate campaign reforms which limited the amount of money that big contributors could spend on political campaigns, greatly benefited Viguerie, who has proven the master at this game of amassing small contributions. His close association with Colorado brewer Joseph Coors, Nixon administration O.E.O. chief Howard Phillips, Wisconsin advertising executive Paul Weyrich and many others, make Viguerie both central and crucial to the New Right Movement. Viguerie's long range plan is to destroy the Republican Party and replace it with a 'new majority' of alienated blue-collar workers, urban ethnics and 'disgruntled Republican Reaganites' . This is a campaign which is intended to 'save the Western World' and rid America of its many enemies.[120]

To this end, he has organized his own political action organizations, including Phillip's Conservative Digest to publish 'New Majority' issues. It is also Viguerie's lists that are being used by Senator Hatch and The Conservative Caucus's anti-ERA drive.

Despite major ideological differences, the New Right is rhetorically indistinguishable from the 'Old Right' characterized by Ronald Reagan and the John Birch Society. This illusion caused by their very similar stands on almost every social issue, however, masks fundamental differences in tactics. Viguerie argues that conservative Republicanism is 'political poison', an attribute which the New Right is set to overcome:

> "It cannot be marketed because a rigid adherence to the free enterprise system has caused traditional conservatives to overlook an entire segment of the American electorate - the blue collar social conservative - who shares with traditional conservatives an opposition to busing, gun control, abortion and detente. If only conservatives would surrender some of their attachment to free-market economics, and their distrust of labor unions and federal power, ... there would be more than enough agreement between the blue collar workers and the Reaganites to form a powerful new party. I'm willing to make concessions to come to power. That's what a coalition is... We're going to have to be willing to use the government to stimulate the economy more than I think we should in order to get votes." [121]

According to Phillips, there are plenty of votes just waiting to be won over. Phillips, accredited with the formulation of Nixon's 'Southern Strategy' that won the traditionally Democratic South for the G.O.P. in 1968 and 1972, is also linked with National Review publisher William A. Rusher as the two chief publicists of the 'New Majority' vision. Rusher authored 'The Making of The New Majority Party', a book which attempts to demonstrate the inevitability of the G.O.P.'s collapse and replacement by a 'New Majority' coalition.

It is apparent to even Republican traditionalists that this new movement is indifferent to ideology. Instead, they seem to be much more interested in broadcasting a set of opinions to merely drum up support. In the New Right thus far, issues have been consistently subordinated to tactical concerns. How 'power' is most easily achieved and forcefully exercised appear to be the main incentives of the fledgling movement.

These tactics have included the usurpation of any and all convenient 'red flag' issues that can create an emotionally charged decoy for the real problems. Such tactics are especially intended to stir up hostilities among lower-middle class whites. Other problems actually more central to these people's interests, such as unemployment, income security, and the failure of the 'middle class dream' in general, are consistently avoided. As Phillips puts it, "we're going after people on the basis of their hot buttons", and thus, emotionally charged issues are unblushingly the target and tactic of the New Right. Viguerie himself states his theory that it is impossible to raise money "unless you conjure up an enemy", seemingly insensitive to the results upon the 'enemy', as long as he raises the money. He also notes that votes are not motivated ideologically, but are only swayed by strong leadership.[122] Not coincidentally, Nazi ideology professed the identical rationale for gaining control over the masses.

Traditional Republican theorists, as would be expected, look upon this opportunist ideology with consternation. As Daniel Joy, legal counsel to Senator James Buckley, notes, such sensationalism of human issues merely feed into "the gnawing suspicion among a good many lower- middle class Americans that somehow, somewhere, something is oppressing them."[123] As such, the New Right is consciously playing upon people' s insecurities, and manipulating these fears to their own advantage. Rogers, for example, enjoys blaming everything on big labor, big business, and the intellectuals. 'The elite is the enemy' is the tactic to simplify and evasively exploit genuine hatred and fear without ever dealing with the concrete issues.

This lashing out at both intellectuals and the business world is glowingly referred to in a 'Conservative Digest' article as " all the pent-up venom of a generation of lower-middle class people who feel betrayed and exploited."[124] This, we must remember, was the very same tactic used by the Nazi right-wing movement to stir up the genuine frustrations of the German lower-middle class, and is most convenient, since the American New Right has no ideology upon which to even attempt to genuinely confront the actual sources of this sense of betrayal and exploitation.

The New Right exhibits a definite preference for conformity and a lack of even minimal tolerance of those whose values or life styles are different, and thus, threatening to their own. As we saw earlier in the case of the Nazi Kampfzeit, or 'Time of Struggle', these are attempts to play upon people's desires for someone to take control and define for them what and who is good and bad, powerful and powerless. This also helps explain Viguerie's personal search over the years to find that certain someone who he calls a man on a white horse to lead the 'New Majority Party.' [125]

Of all these groups and individuals, there is still no charismatic leader for the New Right to coalesce around. Hitler, however, was not that obviously the leader in the beginning of the German Nazi Movement, either. Even after he had taken total control of the rapidly growing Nazi Party, few Germans could believe such a ignoble person could possibly present an actual threat, nor even be taken seriously. He was generally seen as just another 'crank', except by those who were most desperate.

Despite the handicap of being leaderless, the New Right has made extremely significant inroads into the American political power structure. Starting in 1974, the intertwined organizations of Viguerie, the Conservative Caucus, the Committee for the Survival of a Free Congress, and the National Conservative Political Action Committee, have increased the loosely affiliated New Right congressional contingent by 25% in the U.S. Senate, and by more than 25% in the U.S. House of Representatives. This is no small force, and the recent legislative backslide on almost all fronts clearly reflects this growing political force. Among the prime New Right victories in 1976 were those of Utah's Sen. Orrin G. Hatch and California's Sen. S.I. Hayakawa.

The onslaught of the New Right, however, does not end here. As Viguerie so avidly puts it, " I want a massive assault on Congress in 1978. I don't want any token effort. We now have the talents and the resources to move ... against Congress in 1978 in a way that's never been conceived of." [126] Such grand designs seem more than reminiscent of Rev. Moon, and with Viguerie's track record, should not be taken as idle threats.

Will the New Right be successful in replacing the vacuum in the event of a collapse of the Republican Party? Or will the big moneyed interest groups compromise by modifying their defense of the free enterprise system, and resist the extreme right, perhaps even as only a last-ditch effort to maintain some degree of political power? Phillips claims that the blue collar workers, or 'social conservatives', are envious of the government 'handouts' to the poor, or 'unproductive', and must be appeased with a share 'of the pie.' [127] This presents a potent dilemma to the economic control oriented philosophy of the Republican hierarchy, perhaps being equally as important as the intellectual barriers, which are preventing the coalescence of the 'New Majority Party'.

A.F. of L.- C.I.O. President George Meany, in his 1977 Labor Day address, charged that organized labor is the present target of a multi million dollar extremist campaign comparable to the rise of Nazism in prewar Germany. Although he viewed the phenomena from the vested interest position of organized labor, at least Meany's speechwriters appear to see the issues presently threatening America. He stated that a strong and well coordinated business lobby has emerged on Capitol Hill in order to threaten labor legislation, and manipulate public opinion in order to split apart workers and other minorities. He described these 'hate merchants' of the 70's as:

> "slick Madison Avenue types, trained in mass psychology and propaganda techniques, who have computerized mailing lists, a printing press and a government subsidized mailing permit. ... An estimated 150 million letters will be mailed, seeking contributions to fight a host of so-called enemies to the American way of life." [128]

In drawing a parallel to Nazism, Meany continued:

> "Conservatives and some business leaders, who kid themselves into believing they can use the extreme right wing to weaken and eventually destroy organized labor, are playing a dangerous game. They would do well to remember - as we in organized labor remember all too well - what happened to the German industrialists who financed Hitler's Nazi movement because it was pledged to destroy the unions. After turning free unions into a huge, national, compulsory company union - called a Labor Front - Hitler pounced on his industrial supporters, incorporated their plants into his totalitarian system, and reduced the former managers to mere office boys." [129]

VI

CREATING THE NEW

T hroughout this study, the importance of each individual to take his/her power, and the responsibility for it, has been repeatedly demonstrated. The importance of this process becomes more and more critical as humanity finds itself to have come to an impasse' of interrelated dilemmas. In the last century, humanity has experienced major revolutions on almost every level: spiritually, materially, intellectually and emotionally. These changes have been, and are being, accompanied by a heightened pace in the human search for a new meaning and approach to life, and livelihood.

In the old consciousness, however, there is a denial of the fact that the old 'order' of our society is falling apart, as many pretend otherwise, for they don't dare believe it. Others blame foreign or domestic 'enemies', 'the system', 'human nature', or 'fate', and conclude that there is no power on earth that can change 'it'. Such attitudes are cop-outs; failures to be responsible and to trust in one's own ability to choose and act. Pointing fingers elsewhere is only avoiding the issue. We can create the world we want to live in, and this responsibility is not a burden, but liberation itself, for it frees us from self-negating alienation, despair and destructive projection onto others.

171

When any society experiences major upsets or changes in its social fiber, the people within that society can be seen to perceive this change in three basic ways. The first group feels intimidated and insecure following the collapse of their old world, and reacts with distrust, fear and resentment. Their 'success' at submission to external authorities and living behind walls has become a way of life, a perspective from which the world outside is viewed with fear and apprehension, and they are thus thankful for the protection. The derogatory usage of the word 'burgher' illustrates this very well, for the term is used to describe those people whose insecurity is so great that they experience anxiety at the very thought of questioning the control of an external authority, much less of living without it. The derivation of the word is from the German word for 'citizen', or someone who lived in the 'burgs', or walled city/fortresses of medieval Europe. Most of these walls have crumbled with time, only to have been replaced by a multitude of symbolic, but no less limiting walls of self-conception, such as being 'normal', rich, a Wasp, a Doctor, or even an American.

The second group also lacks individual responsibility and awareness of the dynamics that are taking place. Characteristically, this group is often the most severely controlled by the old order, and, as such, has never had much opportunity to learn to internalize self-control. Unlike the first, this second group is primarily composed of minority persons who have never gained much from the old order, and therefore had little or no faith in it. With no one to say "no" anymore, this group tends to use their new 'freedom' as a license to do as they please, going to the extreme in all that they do, just for the unique and withheld experience of it.

Fortunately, there is also a third group consisting of those who have internalized responsibility and were aware of the oppression of the old order. These individuals rejoice at the fall of the old order, and busy themselves with the opportunity/obligation to create new and more meaningful societal institutions and ways of living. However, since the second group tends to act out all the fears of the burghers in their attitude of "there's no one to catch me", the more extreme of these two groups tend to attack one another. Nonetheless, the third group, if it is aware, centered and collectively organized enough to survive, formulates the new societal changes, and after the initial conflict, these changes are eventually incorporated into the entire society.

Since individuals of the third group have already changed themselves, have revolted against the oppression within themselves and without, they experience less stress when the structure of the external order collapses around them. To these people, change is not new, or something to fear. It is this evolutionary force of the self-responsible, rebellious and those who have dared to throw off the old yoke of oppressive roles and values, who form the vanguard of change. Included in this group would be the people personally involved in the spiritual, political, moral and cultural revolutionary movements preceding and initiating the social changes.

Post World War I Germany experienced precisely such social changes, and as we saw in the last chapter, a very similar situation exists in America today. The new consciousness movements of the sixties were the beginning of a major collective search for new direction. It turned vast segments of the population away from the sterile, corporate materialism and the structured, mechanistic 'order', and towards a more human cause. It was also typified by the tension, insecurity and polarization typical of societies undergoing major changes in their fabric. The rumblings of the sixties, of course, were merely the beginnings of the changes which have not come to completion.

The general populace has a long way to go before the concrete realization of what is actually happening becomes widespread enough to collectively manifest the needed changes. Even for those who have rejected many restrictions of the old, there is still a need for a great deal of personal growth if we are to be able to adapt to the new. Although it is apparent that a definite change in our thinking and world view is developing, no one can pretend to know what the specific nature of these changes is for everyone. If change

173

is to be created, we will each need to use our own talents and the lessons from our individual and collective life experiences to find our own unique contributions, whatever forms they may take.

As yet, we do not know all the answers needed to create these changes, for we are still in the process of creating the alternatives. We do know, however, that many aspects of ourselves and our societal organizations cannot continue without disastrous results. We also know that important to this process of change is the need to realize that we cannot wait for some external authority to tell us 'how', or to show us 'the way', for this is the very pitfall of the old authoritarian way.

It is, first of all, everyone's own personal choice as to whether each of us wants to take responsibility for the changes needed in order to realize our visions of a society which has overcome the disadvantages of the past. Secondly, it will only be through consciously overthrowing the fascism within ourselves that we can simultaneously reflect this vision upon the collective level, thereby changing our society as a whole. Since we must each personally find our own meaningful answers, it would be absurd to present the reader with any magical solutions or answers. We can, however, draw some general criteria for creating the new from our study this far. The following, then, are some recommendations resulting from our experience in the old age. These recommendations are intended to be a guide-line, which, it is hoped, will be of assistance in the individual's process of supporting personal and collective growth and evolution.

Although constantly denying one another, the pure political and religious dogmatists have much more in common than either would care to believe. The need for a structured set of rules, an enemy and a leader, are common to both. If we are interested in the synthesis of the existing dichotomies in the creation of the new, then the wide chasm that presently exists between politics and spirituality in the movements, is a phenomenon that must bear close examination.

There is a tendency in the present political movements of the left, in their single-minded concern with economic issues, to leave the entire question of psychological alienation, to the various religious and spiritual movements. In contrast to the political left, which tends to see all in terms of material issues, most of the spiritual movements ignore the political realities completely, often only offering simplistic changes in consciousness that are isolated and confined to only the personal level of existence. Politics is seen by these people as something cold, mechanistic, impersonal and irrelevant to one's inner needs. Such attitudes, of course, are the result of a sense of politics which has lost its human touch, and does not promote individual creative growth and expression. Human proportions have often been lost to such an extent that it tends to adequately represent no individual person.

The great majority of people, however, have a common source of interest in both politics and spirituality; often as a result of discontent with the quality of life that they are experiencing. Unfortunately, religions too often project the solutions inward, and politics project the solutions outward, each to the exclusion of the reality of the other. The individual is confronted with the choice of accepting all of the blame for their situation, as in "the mind creates all", or none of it, as in "victim of oppression." In themselves, both perspectives are escapist, for neither realistically faces the totality of the human experience.

When the political left sees spirituality as nothing more than the fired and dangerous dogma of the Pope, and the spiritual left sees politics as nothing more than the useless task of choosing between two crooks for the presidency, then they each defeat their own purpose. Not only do the two most vital groups able to create meaningful change fail to support each other, they dissipate vital energy as well by opposing each other.

This problem was also present in pre-Nazi Germany, where idealistic counter-cultural movements consistently ignored either the political or spiritual realities of their time. Much as in present-day America, the German youth rediscovered the ancient wisdom of the East. Books such as those of Hermann Hesse, and articles in magazines like the 'The Free German Youth', depicted the searching spirit of those times, spreading Eastern knowledge until the concepts of Karma, yoga, Buddhism and meditation were widespread. New spiritual movements, along with their prophets and gurus, spread like wildfire. Common to all of these movements, however, was an attitude which was basically apolitical.[130]

This more spiritually identified side of the German counter-culture revolted against human alienation, industrialism, materialism and corrupt politics, with poetry, youth festivals, guitars, communal living, long hair and wreaths of flowers in an attempt to spread the ideology of love and peace, primarily through appeals to spirit and emotion. At the same time, the equally vast, and perhaps better organized political left revolted against the same conditions, yet with a more complicated ideology based upon an appeal to the mind and a material analysis. An analysis of the economic exploitation of the working class by the ruling class, to the exclusion of the more subtle oppression, gained vast intellectual and youthful support that was at least as extensive, if not more so, than in America today. Its tendency towards theoretical rhetoric, however, failed to attract a broad enough base, even within the working class itself, and tended to alienate the middle class, as well as the ruling class. In the end, both groups failed to incorporate the personal and collective dilemma, into a realistic and united movement in opposition to the Nazi reactionary alternative.

The somewhat naively spiritually-oriented German youth did not realize that by personally defying the authoritarian and materialistic system through their alternative lifestyles, and defying traditional roles, they were, in fact, making strong political statements. This oblivion, however, was not destined to spare them from the consequences of these statements in the least. While the spiritual movements refused to 'stoop' to the base level of external politics, searching for internal meaning instead, the political left did not find it economically relevant to attend to the psychological yearnings of their spiritually-oriented peers, much less those of the populace as a whole. They failed to understand the importance of the phenomena of striving for inner meaning amidst external alienation, a tactic that the Nazis did not overlook. Because of this, the Nazis were unchallenged in their infiltration and cooption of much of the idealistic, yet politically naive, spiritual/utopian realm, selling their movement as a spiritual revolution as much as a political one.

The results of this tragic lack of unity, however, could have been avoided. Both in true politics and spirituality, there is a heightened sense of self-awareness which can be used to understand reality both inside and outside of the self. It is this harmonious balance and synthesis between the internal/external, spiritual/political, which is the dynamic factor in our personal and collective growth towards wholeness. Without this synthesis, politics tends to become impersonal and alienating, and spirituality self-indulgent and oblivious to others.

The political left basically consists of individuals dedicated to the responsible social interaction between individuals in an attempt to create collective situations which are most advantageous for all involved. The spiritual left or counter-culture is composed of individuals dedicated to the improvement of human existence by supporting the personal development of a deeper understanding of personal power, needs and direction, and thus, the creation of a truly personalized meaning to life. In effect, we can see each is 'opposite' only in that each looks at the same goal from the opposite perspective: either from that of the personal or that of the collective. As such, they are both integral parts of the same whole, for one cannot be achieved without the other. Collective/external happiness cannot be gained without the awareness of personal/internal happiness, and personal happiness cannot be achieved without an awareness of how one's actions effect others, and thus effect the collective well being. The fullest possible personal/collective growth and development is, hopefully, the aim of both perspectives. Within this holistic context of the human experience, we can see how one's politics can be the external reflection of one's inner spirituality, and vice-versa. Both the internal and external dimensions of one's nature are thus seen as being equally important, for our self-conceptions and our abilities to respect other's are intricately intertwined.

The separation of Church and State is essential for any democracy. However, a synthesis of the political and spiritual components of a counter-culture, is not only possible, but imperative if it is to fully succeed. Spiritual groups must become actively aware of the political dimensions of their activities, and political movements, for their part, must not allow themselves to become cold, impersonal and mechanistic structures which are solely interested in the material struggles for control of the economic pie. No escapes into an ashram, the organic woods, political dogma, drugs, music or leaders can spare us from the reality of the immense struggle and conflict that now permeates our entire society. Of course, Atheists are also a part of the mix, and have every right to be heard and respected. Only through collective efforts to consciously integrate alternatives to both the external and internal chaos of our alienated society, will the drift to the totalitarian right be countered by a unified movement that is able to materialize its dreams of a society in which the individual well being and the collective well being are truly synonymous.

PERSONAL CONSIDERATIONS

One very important factor in this process of creating the new is the need for people to stop 'asking' for their freedom and personal power. No one can 'give' us our freedom or personal power. We must, individually and collectively, take it. By begging for something that cannot be in the possession of some external authority, we are only creating an illusion and a trap. Furthermore, if someone in the external can 'give' us our freedom and personal power, then that same source can just as easily take it away. Any such projections into the external leaves us in an insecure position. Although this concept is not a magical cure-all, the assumption that

178

we already have freedom and power, puts us in a much stronger position to start from, in combating external and internal oppression.

It is also important to be able to differentiate between 'an answer' and 'the answer'. 'The answer' for everyone is not at all likely to be found in any one political or religious doctrine or 'ism'. Too much emotional attachment and identification with any one ideology is restrictive, in that it inherently is not conducive to independent or holistic thinking. Rather, the goal is a synthesis of what is currently relevant from all these movements, past and present, for there are important principles to be learned from all the major political and religious movements.

We should also remember that within each of us is an energy which goes far beyond any one cultural, racial, religious or political orientation. Although it is important to speak out and confront the views of others in order to manifest our own principles, this zeal must be tempered by an awareness that the ultimate goal is the growth and happiness of all humanity, in all its variety.

Despite the fact that an alienated sense of security is gained by creating an enemy, it takes a lot more security to go out of one's own reality in order to understand those of others. By trying to understand these other realities, or actually putting oneself in another's place, we can realize that no one person or group is totally 'evil' or destructive, but is merely doing what they have learned, from their own life experiences, seems right for themselves. This perspective of being open to other's realities can much more easily lead to a mutual understanding and exchange. It can also result in not only a constructive settlement of seemingly 'opposing' views and interests, but in both party's personal growth as well.

In blaming any person or group as the source of 'evil', we are actually attempting to escape our own responsibilities, which include the well-being of the greater whole of humanity, as well as of the individual self. By making those who have come to a different conclusion, most likely based upon entirely different life experiences, into an 'enemy', we seek to avoid our responsibility to them as another part of humanity. Seeing people as only 'gooks', 'queers', 'commies', or 'rednecks', is the most convenient method of avoiding understanding the development of their perspective. It is, after all, the only one they have, and it will not be changed through intimidation.

The fact is that we can all be free, independent and, yet still, an integral part of collective humanity. Through the realization of one's self-power, it also becomes clear that everyone else can have self-power, as long as this self-power is not used as a weapon against others.

The need for an enemy is irrational and life-negating, in that inevitably some portion of humanity will have to become this enemy, and we all know what happens to 'the enemy'. In exactly the same manner, we cannot allow ourselves the convenience of seeing the 'new right', the 'burghers', or the 'rednecks' as 'the enemy' either. Instead, we can see them as people with very different life experiences, in which the internalization of their oppression meant survival in the only sense in which they could imagine it. The fact that often they themselves do not perceive that they are oppressed, or that they have accepted societal scapegoats, cannot be allowed to obscure the fact that they still very much feel the hurt, however suppressed the symptoms. Unless their very real feelings of alienation and powerlessness are acknowledged, as well as their capacity for growth and change, just as our own, then the specter of the 'New Right' is the only logical alternative. When the time comes that we can no longer respect one another's existence, then we can no longer respect ourselves either, and we are experiencing our own destruction.

In the past, anyone who was physically, emotionally, mentally or sexually different than the prevailing order was either subdued, destroyed or had to flee into such institutions as the military or the monastery. Without this desperate need to escape somewhere, anywhere, such institutions of power would never have managed to attract so many young people, or have become so powerful.

Times, however, are changing. As our society experiences these at times disruptive changes, more and more people are becoming aware of self-power, as they finally begin using it. Indeed, the self is more powerful than formerly suspected. Individuals are learning to rely upon their own resources, particularly the lessons of their own personal experiences and common sense. Many people are realizing that they are capable of knowing what is best for themselves. People are beginning to question the experts and officials on their 'authority' as the only ones with the last word or the inside information. They are no longer feeling small and incapable, no longer needing to look up to the vested powers for guidance and external control. These changes in the temperament and consciousness of the people are seriously threatening the existing structure, which fears nothing more than a populace capable of alert and independent thinking. We are realizing that we no longer need to be mindless, non-thinking workers and consumers, who believe and do only that which is told to us from above. We now can understand that the great laws and truths of the universe are not that complicated. One of the most basic of these laws is that each person is solely responsible for their actions and the consequences of these actions, and is thus, the dispenser of happiness or gloom upon oneself. In other words, to a certain extent, we decree our lives, our rewards and our self-destruction, on whichever level we choose. At the same time realizing that this personal process is greatly affected by the collective process, which often molds our very conception of happiness and rewards.

We are beginning to realize at an increasing rate, that things do not need to be as complicated and mystifying as we had been led to believe. This change in attitude and awareness is creating a human experience which is no longer narrow, restricted and isolated. We are becoming less and less susceptible to those in our society who represent the authoritarian principles, and who have been long aware of the subtle ways through which one gains control of the masses of people. The old formulae which employ guilt and fear just are not working as well anymore.

A direct result of this increase in awareness and consciousness, is that it has powerful political overtones, especially so since an increase in personal power should also result in the realization that each individual has immense political power, as well as a responsibility for how it is used collectively.

One of the most important and powerful steps an individual can make in his/her progress towards self-power is to take control of what s/he does for work, and how s/he does it. Today, the vast majority of people have no control over even the most immediate level of the economic machine, and have little chance of ever developing genuine relatedness and purposefulness at their jobs. They are 'employed', and nothing more is expected of them but to obey their employers, in the service of vast material empires which need police states, armament races and imperialistic oppression to support them. If it is not our responsibility to change this situation, then whose is it? If some seventy million Americans begrudgingly and mechanically get up every morning to dehumanizing work, it is frightful to think of the amount of negative psychic energy these people are putting into the collective consciousness, not to mention what it is doing to their own psyches.

Humans need to become the masters of the social and economic forces, not the slaves. The opportunity for creative intelligent and shared responsibility can be regained. People can define their own conception of 'work', as well as its requirements, and still contribute to the overall growth and well being of the collective grouping. The current term for this process is 'right livelihood', and centers have sprung up which support people to take the responsibility to make their fulfillment of material needs consistent with their own personal values.

Economically, when capitalism is no longer expanding through colonization, imperialism and wars, there are not enough 'jobs' for everyone, no matter how alienating. It would therefore, seem logical that we not only need to allow people to create more meaningful 'work', but we also have to create an economic system that is not based upon exploitation, oppression and 'more is better'.

In fact, intrinsic to the creation of such a system, will be the need to sacrifice some of what we have been sold as material 'necessities', in order to actually come to a tangible conception of 'less is more'. Yet, forced communism, as in the example of the Soviet Union, can easily be deceptive, for although collectivization of the means of production has taken place, actually a powerful bureaucracy still manipulates and controls the masses of people, who are still enslaved to the work machine of a huge empire.

The fact is, that all of these huge and powerful systems are dominated by a compulsive drive to produce an array of mechanical gadgetry, from armaments to spray deodorants, few of which are basic to human survival. At present, we possess the technical know-how to produce far more than enough of the essential needs for all people on the entire planet. This could be, that is, if people were not conditioned to want a vast assortment of material substitutes for their own lack of personal fulfillment.

Only when people have time and energy beyond the satisfaction of their primary needs, can they begin to pursue personal growth and enrichment on levels other than amassing material objects. Yet, this is impossible if people are caught up in the work syndrome, which is necessary in order to obtain external gratification. We must learn to recognize that the common goals of money, ambition, status and power are traps that torment us with servitude to material goods and consumerism. These are fraudulent substitutes for a richness in life that is not only dependent upon the material level of existence. Once people realize this fact, and incorporate it into their lifestyles, then a major portion of their enslavement will have been removed. We need to reorient ourselves to the question of what the individual really needs for happiness and fulfillment. It is the growth of people, after all, that matters, rather than just a material form of 'progress'.

Another important change which the individual can incorporate into his/her world view is an understanding of natural sexuality. Due to extensive authoritarian conditioning, this process is often most difficult, and therefore, even more crucial for each individual to accomplish. Natural sexuality, we have seen, is a contradiction, and even a threat, to the patriarchal tradition which teaches us to 'conquer' and negate much of our sexuality. Yet, in loathing ourselves and our basic animal nature, as well as associating natural sexuality with 'sin', we are weakening our self-image and self-power. Indirectly, we then also create the need for scapegoats, or 'bad' people who do not live up to the standards of 'normalcy'. Notions of 'abnormality', whether in reference to race, sanity, gender, appearance, or sexual preference can no longer be accepted. Human equality means that all people have a claim and right to freedom and happiness. What is does not mean, however, is that all people are alike. Diversity is life, and the destruction of variety is death, as we saw demonstrated in Nazi Germany.

Authoritarianism, whether of the left or of the right, is the political expression of a morbid fear of variation; a life-denying need for uniformity. In fact, there is a wide range of choices by which people can identify, secure that the masculine/feminine interaction within each individual is not only normal, but the dynamic factor in one's wholeness. There is an urgent need for humans to realize the oneness of the female/male dynamics within each person; a concept that is both spiritually ancient and scientifically modern.

Individuals can learn to know and understand their own meaningfulness and purpose without imitating pre-fabricated stereotypical roles and ideas. We do not have to be extensions of an automaton society. Rather, we can, if we choose, take opportunities to leave behind any oppressive situations of an external or internal nature. If people around us cannot be themselves, and if we cannot be ourselves around them, then games are being played. Our option is to drop both the games and the people if necessary, for we can find a space where people's lives and lifestyles are more in tune with who we are. We now can perceive that we are in control, and responsible for ourselves and our universe. We can change the nature of ourselves and thus our interactions.

It is advantageous for us to express ourselves, both our pains and our joys. We cannot relate to others unless we let them know who and what we ourselves are, and if we don't know, then that is communicated as well. We do not have to apologize for ourselves anymore, but instead we can use that energy to become what it is that we desire to be. Anyone who adds nothing to our lives, or wants to control us, or us to control them, can be avoided. It is no longer our game, and the only way to 'win' is to refuse to play it, and that, is personal power.

In being open to genuine communication, we are more capable of discerning and choosing with whom we wish to share. We can then, authentically and without manipulation, be close to others and feel a sense of community. In doing so, we can open dimensions of ourselves which alienation had banished from our awareness. The child in each of us becomes strong again, as we allow ourselves to feel, laugh, cry, play, relate and express.

To those still held captive in the old, the person who has taken his/her power and the responsibility for it, will certainly stand out. People within the old are not used to witnessing a whole person living as an integrated and expressive individual outside of the restrictions of 'normal' life, and may perceive him/her in a range from adoration, to 'weird', or even as a threat.

Such insecurity is in all of us to a certain extent, especially when we first begin striking out on our own. Many people go through a difficult period when making the transition from the old to the new. This is only natural in view of the amount of conditioning which we have to unlearn. To unlearn many of the desires and goals which have been implanted in us is not easy, and does not happen over-night. There is usually a lot of resentment, emotional conflict, inhibitions, fear and guilt which must be resolved in this process of unlearning the old patterns of restriction and self-negation. Nonetheless, it is important to confront and release what lies below the defenses which we have all learned in order to survive in the old. Therefore, the need for supportive communities of growth-conscious people, where individuals are not treated as a threat, and not forced into 'roles'.

We must learn to stop hiding our pains and frustrations, thereby allowing others to show theirs as well. In being afraid, we fear ourselves as well as each other. When we can love ourselves, then, and only then, are we capable of loving others. We cannot betray our abilities to love and share. Alienation, guilt and fear can be unlearned by consciously claiming that which we want to be, and then becoming it. The changes which we engender in our culture and society are also reflected in our language. Languages, as all else, are always in the process of changing and growing. For example, as a society becomes more fascistic, its language reflects this in its regimentation, restriction and life-negation. A language can only reflect the consciousness of the people who use it, and due to hundreds of years of authoritarian control, our languages no longer reflect the consciousness of many of the people, and must be changed. Words, thought forms, phrases and idioms which have negative connotations and references to powerful/powerless, superior/inferior, defensiveness, etc. are no longer needed.

Words are a vehicle of communication, and whether it is our intention or not, when we use words of a racist, sexist or otherwise oppressive nature, we, in fact, communicate oppression. Removing such modes of speech and replacing them with more appropriate ones, not only reflects our changed reality, but also serves to support, rather than oppress others. As with most changes, we should not wait for a revolution of dictionary makers, for these are our words, not theirs.

COLLECTIVE CONSIDERATIONS

In this period of transition, it is important for us to channel our energies into creating the new, rather than dissipating our energies in the near hopeless task of reforming the old. In trying to reform the old, however noble our intentions, we usually end up losing our incentive and impetus, because we are allowing the old system/structure to define the area and context of whatever it is we

186

are trying to change. Creating the new within the severe constraints of the old, or 'healing it', is a self-defeating and often impossible task, as many people have already found out. Of course, we need our institutions, and there is no need to abandon them. However, other than Whistle Blowers coming forward from within an institution, and initiating a review in order to spur change, the institution itself, rarely changes of its own volition. Rather, the institution will usually only change when forced to by the people it serves. Once these changes have been made, they can be monitored by creating independent Review Boards of the various professions and institutions, providing much needed oversight.

Naive idealism urges us to attempt to reform the old structure, for it would be so simple to change this one little thing, and it makes so much sense. However, when confronted with the vested interests of the old order, it is hard not to feel defeated, and to then withdraw alone or acquiesce. This can lead to thankfulness for only token changes, and leave us open to constant cooptation by 'rewards' to 'join the system'. The problem here is often a lack of awareness that these various struggles are not isolated. Real change cannot come about in any one area without it serving to threaten the entire system. The old order, therefore, will not give up without a tremendous fight.

A powerful alternative, is to take what can be helpful from the old, and then withdraw our energies from it, for it is unwilling to change, it is already in the death- throws of its own destruction. Instead, we can channel our energies into creating the new. This does not mean, however, that we are unaware or insensitive to the plight of those still caught within the old order. No, we must be supportive and understanding of them, helping them to make the transition to the new as well. By creating new centers and communities, we can offer concrete alternatives which can serve as support, inspiration, incentive and direction for those still within the old, who need more than theory.

The great advantage of such materialized liberation movements and support groups, is that they can provide an environment supportive of the integration of personal growth with the search for political/spiritual change. Such groupings can provide mutual therapy from within, without needing to wait for the rest of society to change. These groups are not waiting for the intangible 'promised land', or 'the revolution', but are busy creating their visions and dreams. In this way, we can inaugurate change by offering ourselves as concrete examples for those in the old, rather than merely reacting by condemning them and 'their' society.

In a sense, this transition into the new is a form of anarchy, as we discard the old ways for the spontaneity of the new. Anarchy is not a goal in itself, but merely a process which is an integral part of evolutionary change, both in personal and collective growth. This process cannot be avoided, for we cannot create the new until we have let go of the old. Thus, a holistic concept of change would include anarchy as a process within the whole cycle of change and evolution, as a tool rather than a weapon. Anarchy as a goal, needless to say, is to be avoided at all costs.

At present, we live in a society which is ruled by super-structures which control both the social and economic forces. In their efforts to control every level of the dynamics of our society, the use of force has become an everyday occurrence. By externally imposing laws upon people, such systems take for granted that people are, by and large, incapable of personal discretion, and are unable to decide for themselves what course of action would be most beneficial at a given moment or situation. Before we wake up to find ourselves in a society which has become a prison, a technologically ordered hell, as happened to so many in Nazi Germany, we must firmly establish a society based upon human freedom, where no one authority is allowed such pervasive power.

The active control and cooperation of each individual, and by the smallest communities or groups in the whole system, will require a degree of decentralization. Although the state may have originally been identical with society, it has now become alienated from society and functions largely as a power above and often against the people. People now need to learn not to rely upon these huge, depersonalized power structures, be they the state or church of whatever brand. Such mammoth organizations, by their very nature, cannot possibly be sensitive to the common people's real needs as they see them. As we have continually seen, there is also a dangerous tendency for alienated people to hide behind the 'greatness' of these external powers.

In order to gain a planetary spirit in which one sees his/her country to symbolically include the entire planet, it will be necessary to organize social structures which do not alienate, mitigate or destroy individual power. The need to identify with external powers will no longer need to be encouraged, as authoritarian leadership is replaced by humanistic structures which support and teach self-regulation in society.

The organization of communities, neighborhoods and support groups can serve a great function in this process of decentralization, since they can help return political interaction to a human scale. Such communities can function within the context of human proportions, in which each member can be an integral and informed part of the social and economic process.

This organization of the social, political, economic and spiritual structures can also be helpful to people who are in the process of learning to take their personal power and the responsibility for that power, as well as to assist them in relearning a sense of spontaneity within a modern context. Smaller groups, societies, or tribes, functioning within the larger collective whole is an ancient practice, common to all of humanity. As such, there is a rich historical and multi-cultural background from which we can develop new applications.

Communities can develop their own community services on economic, political, social and spiritual levels. From food co-ops, and growing organic food, to solar energy, the organization of largely self-sufficient groups will help create an environment where people no longer need to feel isolated from one another, and totally dependent upon super power structures. Such communities can also develop applications of modern technology which are most appropriate, and least harmful, to individual well being, and to the environment. Solar energy is an excellent example of this application of technology for the true benefit of all the people. Once installed, it costs very little to produce energy, since everyone has free access to the sun. Indeed, solar energy has been denied us by the economically powerful precisely because it could not be monopolized and sold for excessive profit.

We can also liberate ourselves from the control of powerful religions without losing anything of value. Humans have a natural religious or spiritual inheritance which is not dependent upon any hierarchical power structure. This spirituality, as seen within the context of human evolution, as well as its relation to the direction and purpose of all of life, has been built stratum-like upon the older levels of human wisdom without becoming the property of any particular institutional representatives. For example, the ancient Hermetic Principles display an awareness of universal law which is astoundingly simple, yet in many ways parallels modern theories.

In this ancient knowledge, it is stated that not only does the mind create, but that everything is also pulsating energy. This presents the possibility of our understanding reality in terms of energy, rather than in terms of material objects. Hence, energy and/or life can be seen in all things, from stones to water; all are pulsating electrical vibrations of energy. This gives us a new understanding of life and its meaning, as all is now perceivable as life, a concept central to Native Americans world views. This concept should then change our old belief in the myth that humans are 'superior' to other forms of life, and the masters/conquers of nature. In this new concept, life and nature are one. Nature becomes our great teacher and benefactor, and any notion of 'conquering' it becomes absurd.

Like the North American Hopi, we too can learn that happiness, power and prosperity go beyond materialism, and cannot be measured by mere physical dimensions. This tribe chose the wasteland desert to live in, in order to avoid invasions and wars.

On this land, to the amazement of agricultural officials, they have grown lush crops from a climate and soil which would normally produce next to nothing. These peaceful people have remembered the essence of human magic and power, and have much to teach us. Indeed, we need to slow down and remember who we are. Communities functioning with the purpose of the common growth of all its members will no longer need to exaggerate the importance of the nuclear family. Rather, the whole group becomes 'family', in which there are many mothers, fathers, brother, sisters, etc., and gender roles can become more relaxed. This is a concept which many Native Americans understood and is one which our society as a whole has only recently forgotten. This is not to say that there is no place for the nuclear family, but it does imply a broadening of our concept of family, which includes the nuclear family.

Although we all have been raised in the patriarchy, we can, nonetheless, create situations in which the principles of matriarchy are reinstated, creating a much needed balance. We create our concepts of family and gender roles. They are not preordained, for indeed, the concept of family is changing. The blood bond is losing hold; we are beginning to understand that we are all one family, no matter what our last names may be. Women's liberations movements, rebellious youth movements and the growth of liberation movements on the parts of men, Gays, and the elderly, are increasingly undermining the age old tyranny of patriarchy. In contrast to the authoritarian hierarchy, the new goal is to support the development of self-directed individuals in active relationship to their environment. On the societal level, these small groupings of people can more easily reflect the perceived needs of their members.*

'No matter how alluring the simplicity, we cannot return to any system of the past, for we are not in the past. Rather, we are creating something new, something beyond our present societal systems, a new synthesis'. For more ideas how this might develop, an inspirational source is Marge Piercys Woman on the Edge of Time. (Knopf, New York, 1976)

As one example, making decisions which will affect the whole, within the context of these smaller groupings, allows the use of more constructive processes. The use of consensus in decision making can help avoid authoritarian tendencies, or the discrimination against any one group. In majority rule, there is a strong tendency to ignore the opinions of minorities, for their support is inherently unnecessary, often resulting in a tyranny of the majority. In contrast, consensus decision making does not require that everyone hold the same belief, but only that everyone agree to consent to abide by a united plan of action. Such consensus starts from a premise that everyone holds the collective welfare foremost, and the interaction is based upon mutual trust rather than mistrust or suspicion. Thus, each participant's views are respected. Not only does this process insure that all opinions are freely aired and reconciled, but that any decided course of action will carry the united spirit of all the members. Although our society instills in us suspicion of one another's motives, and hence alienation from one another, this process of consensus works surprisingly well at not only arriving at decisions, but also at restoring mutual respect and trust.

Lastly, the role of education and of institutions in general, must be to assist individuals in the process of their own self realization. Inherent within this thinking is that love and respect cannot be imposed upon anyone, nor given to anyone. Rather, they must be collectively and personally nurtured within everyone for everyone. This must include a respect for oneself, for one cannot have respect for others until one has learned self-respect. The Eastern greeting Namaste, or "I honor the spirit within you," eludes to this instinctive respect for others. Accepting one another's humanity and genuinely understanding others, rather than merely tolerating them, is an essential principle of a just society, including respect for other forms of life and the balance of nature; the greater whole.

Education can be seen as a lifelong concern, not just for the youth, and not only defined by degrees or titles. Instead, everyone can be seen as a teacher, and also as a student. Our concept of learning can then include a holistic concept of wisdom, rather than continue our preoccupation with genius and specialization alone. Equally important as knowing all there is to know in one specific area, is the ability to understand how each piece fits into the greater whole of knowledge. Individuals can therefore, be taught not to fear their minds, or their ability to understand the unique meaning and purposefulness of their lives. The mind is seen as an important tool which assists us in the process of self-realization, or self-wisdom, rather than merely providing a ticket for an external goal, like a job that has nothing to do with personal development.

If any one question is crucial to the creation of a new and better society, however, it is whether people are willing to grow, change and gain self- power by taking the responsibility for it. If people are strong enough, a collective situation of mutual growth and respect can be created, which in turn, can be reflected in our institutions and society in general. If, on the other hand, people avoid the whole issue, they will, in all likelihood, be lead, controlled and restricted by forces outside of themselves, much like it has been in the past. Change is growth, if we do not fear it. Change is painful, destructive and negative, if we fear it. Either way, change is bound to happen. The choice is ours!

EPILOGUE

Since this book was written there have been, and are many examples of fascism at work. We have had the development of the extreme right-wing Tea Party of the Republican Party, causing a dangerous increase in the polarization of American politics. There have been two botched wars, the Iraq and Afghanistan wars, both initiated and justified on questionable grounds, with negative results all around. The financial crisis of 2008-2009 further exasperated the already declining middle and working classes, increasing the widening gap between the rich and the poor.

Fortunately, there has been a push back. The Occupy Wall Street Movement has done much to expose the corruption and accesses of the powerful banks and corporations. Scandals have been made public; from the Snowden revelations of NSA spying, to the Catholic Church's clergy sexual abuse scandal and its cover up. The shameful legacy of Residential Schools and its abuse of Aboriginal First Nation's children has been exposed to the public. People are no longer in the dark, and are beginning to question authorities. The general degradation of the environment, which we all depend upon for our very existence, is finally being addressed, and people are demanding action be taken by our governments and leaders. There has been a massive grassroots organized resistance to more pipelines, fracking and LNG plants. The proposed Enbridge Northern Gateway Pipeline would run through B.C.'s Great Bear Rainforest threatening this precious natural resource of unspoiled Canadian wilderness, increasing tanker traffic, and potential oil spills along the West Coast. This in itself would be a travesty, but the impact on First Nation's food supply and economy would be equally disastrous.

The role of the internet in disseminating information on an unprecedented scale, has helped spawn and fuel social change across the globe. There have been inspirational revolutionary movements in the Middle East, toppling corrupt regimes, one after the other, with the people demanding more just and equitable societies. The internet, unfortunately, has also helped the spread of extremists through the radicalization of vulnerable young people. Radical right-wing Islamic groups have found fertile recruiting grounds through the use of the internet to influence and brainwash young people into becoming self sacrificing Jihadist terrorists. Other right-wing groups, such as the White Supremists have also used the internet to spread their venom of fear and hatred.

Nonetheless, there is much to be hopeful about. Many young people are stepping up to the plate, and are responding with innovative solutions to our most urgent and pressing problems, such as the need for renewable energy sources and a cleaner environment. In the post 2008-2009 world, many of them no longer strive for the goals of their parents. They seek meaningful work, and as a result are promoting the growth of a purpose driven economy. They are adjusting to a new reality. They are not giving up! Savvy in the use of digital technology, they are on the cutting edge of change, and are helping to formulate a new society based on the new realities of today. This may well be part of the development of a new paradigm, ushering in a major shift in our thinking about our place in the world, and ultimately changing society forever.

People who long for the past, 'the good old days', are sadly deluded. As Rose Braude, a dear Friend of mine, used to say: "they were not good, they were the 'bad old days'. People were mean in the old days." She was an African American who grew up in Louisiana long before Civil Rights, and all the progress that was to come. She knew perfectly well how nasty people were back in the old days. Yes, things have improved since then. Humans are evolving. Freedom is rising! Self-empowered people are everywhere! But much work is yet to be done in order to rid and heal ourselves, and the world, of the destructive violent legacy left by fascism. Foremost, in this effort, is the creation of a non- authoritarian society.

As we have seen in the analysis of fascism, the wealthy one percent, including many large corporations and banks, all too often support fascistic organizations and individuals. People such as the Koch brothers, Charles and David Koch who support right- wing interests from the GOP to the oil and gas industries, through various advocacy and lobbying organizations, and at the same time, oppose universal health care, and climate change legislation. It is time to end the tyranny of the few, the one percent, who hold all the cards in a system rigged in their favor, from controlling the destiny of the masses. This one percent's influence has corrupted our democracies to the point that our governments are on the brink of becoming Oligarchies.

We desperately need a society where aggression, violence, environmental destruction, and war- like posturing are no longer the norm. Rather, we need harmony and peace, where healing and fairness can take place on a large scale. We need a society where attributes such as empathy, kindness and compassion for others, are an accepted integral part of everyday life. It may be high-minded, and idealistic sounding, but it is a goal worth pursuing. I believe it is a goal essential to our survival, and to that of our environment.

—FOOTNOTES—

1. Wilhelm Reich," Massen Psychologie des Faschismus" (The Albion Press, 1970), p. 21.

2. Ibid., p. 22.

3. T.W. Adorno Else Frenkel-Brunswick, Daniel J. Levison and R. Nevitt Stanford, "The Authoritarian Personality" (W.W. Norton & Co., Inc., New York, 1969), pp.365-6

4. Ibid., p. 385

5. Ibid., p. 845 6. Ibid., p. 852.

7. Ibid., p. 475.

8. Ibid., pp. 477-8, 612.

9. Ibid., pp. 477-9.

10. Ibid., pp. 856, 860, 868.

11. Ibid., p. 872.

12. Ibid., pp. 467, 476.

13. Ibid., p. 385.

14. Ibid., p. 850

15. Eric Fromm, " Escape From Freedom" (New York: Rinehart & Co., Inc., 1941), p.19.

16. Op Cit., Adorno, p. 662

17. Op Cit., Fromm, p.215

18. James D. Steakley, 'The Homosexual Emancipation Movement in Germany' (New York: Arno Press, 1975). Jonathan Katz, "Gay American History" (New York: T.Y. Crowell co., 1976), pp. 377—383, 388—390, 395-396.

19. Jill Stephenson, "Women in Nazi Society" (New York: Harper & Row, Barnes and Noble Import Division, printed in England, 1975), pp. 1—10, 27—30, 194—6.

20. Peter D. Stachura, "Nazi Youth in the Weimar Reub1ic" (Santa Barbara, Ca., Oxford, England, Clio Books, 1975), pp. 108-9, 180.

21. Hans Peter Bleuel, "Sex and Society in Nazi Germany"(New York: Bantom Books, 1973, pp. 123-4.

22. Op Cit., Stachura, p. 3.

23. Ibid., pp. 107-111.

24. Ibid., pp. 92 185-192.

25. Karl Dietrich Bracher, "The German Dictatorship, The Origins, Structure and Effects of National Socialism" New York: Draeger Publishers, 1970), pp. 169, 179—81, 202—4, 351, 363.

26. Op Cit., Reich, p. 35.

27. Op Cit., Fromm, pp. 218-19.

28. Op Cit., Reich, pp. 90—91, 93;'O Cit., Stephenson, pp. 27—30, 194-196.

29. Op Cit., Stephenson, pp. 15—16, 194—196.

30. Op Cit., Bleuel, p.9.

31. Op Cit., Reich, p. 51.

32. Op Cit., Bleuel, p.10.

33. Op Cit., Reich, p.33.

34. Op Cit., Bleuel, p. 10.

35. Ibid., P.58

36. Ibid., p. 146.

37. Ibid., p. 185.

38. Op Cit., Fromm, p. 233.

39. Op Cit., Bleuel, p.176.

40. Op Cit., Reich, p. 50.

41. Op Cit., Bleuel, pp.49-50.

42. Charles Reich, "The Sorcerer of Bolinas Reef" (New York; Random House, 1976), p. 217.

43. Barry M. Blechman and Stephen s. Kaplan, "The Use of the Armed Forces as a Politcal Instrument" (The Brookings Institute, Washington, 1977') p. 14.

44. Op Cit., Reich, p.125.

45. Ibid., p. 127.

46. Ibid., p. 126.

47. Derrick Sherwin Bailey, "Homosexuality and the Western Christian Tradition" (New York: Archon Books, 1975), p.70 ; original source: Clyde Pharr, "The Theodosian Code" (Princeton, 1952), pp.231—232.

48. Op Cit., Bracher, pp.386-7.

49. Op Cit., Reich, p. 98.

50. Ibid., p. 197.

51. Op Cit., Adorno, p. 734.

52. Manly P. Hall, "The All-seeing Eye" (Los Angeles: The Hall Publishing Co., Vol.5, 1931), p.1:31.

53. Ibid., p.142.

54. Op Cit., Fromm, p. 60.

55. Ibid., p, 81.

56. Ib1d., p. 82 (taken from Romerbrief, 13.1).

57. Ibid., p. 82 (taken from The Works of Martin Luther, Against the Robbing and Murder Hordes of Peasants, 1525, trans. by G.M0 Jacobs, A.T. Holman Co., Philadelphia, 1931 Vol. X, IX, p.41l).

58. Ibid., p. 84 (John Calvin, "Institutes of the Christian Religion" John Allen, Philadelphia, 1928 Vol. III).

59. Ibid., p.98.

60. Ibid., p.111.

6l. James Goodnow and Barbers Stephens, "Master Speaks" (New York: Citizen's Awareness, translated by Won Pok Choi, 1977), p. 9.

62. Ibid., p.12.

63. Ibid., p.19, ("Master Speaks", delivered on Feb. 4, 1974 on "Indemnity and Unification'.

64. New York Times, Oct. 4, 1977, 63.5.

65. Op Cit., Goodnow-Stephens, p.12.

66. Ibid., p. 6.

67. Ibid., pp. 4, 7, 11 12.

68. New York Times, Oct. 8, 1977, 10.6.

69. 'The Iron Fist And The Velvet Clove,' An Analysis of the U.S. Police, The Center For Research on Criminal Justice, Berkeley, CA, 1975, p.7; original source: U.S. Department of Justice, Law Enforcement Assistance Administration,' Trends in Expenditure and Employment Data for the Criminal Justice System,'1971-1974, Washington D.C., U.S. Government Printing Office, 1976, pp. 2-3;Center for National Security Studies, "Law and Disorder," IV, Washington D.C., Center for National Security Studies, 1976, p.3.

70. Ibid., p. 9.

71. Ibid., pp. 20, 21, 26.

72. Ibid., p. 24.

73. Ibid., p. 29.

74. Ibid., p. 26; original source: Eugene Watts, The Police In Atlanta, 1890- 1903, Journal of Southern History, 1972; Allen Grimshaw, Racial Violence in the U.S., Chicago, Aldine, 1969.

75. Ibid., p. 26. .

76. Ibid., p. 28; original source: Richard Maxwell Brown, 'Strain of Violence: Historical Studies of American Violence and Vigilantism," New York, Oxford University Press, 1974.

77. Ibid., p. 43.

78. Ibid. p. 161.

79. Ibid., p. 44; original source: The National Advisory Commission on Civil Disorders, 'Kerner Report', Washington D.C., U.S. Government Printing Office, 1968.

80. Ibid., p. 13; original source: Eric Wright, 'The Politics of Punishment,' New York, Harper and. Row, 1973, pp. 28-30.

81. Ibid., pp. 82-3.

82. Ibid., p. 77 (original source: Kieth L. Warn, "System Engineering Approach to Law Enforcement", S.A. Yefsky, ed., 'Law Enforcement Science and Technology,' Chicago, Thompson Book Co., 1976,p.651).

83. Ibid., p. 33 (original source: Roscoe Pound, 'Criminal Justice in In the American City,' Cleveland, Cleveland Foundation, 1922,p.15)

84. Ibid., p. 50.

85. Ibid., pp. 93-4.

86. Ibid., p.94.

87. Ibid., (original source: Philip S. Foner,ed., 'The Black Panthers Speak,' New York, Lippencott, 1970).

88. Ibid., p. 97.

89. Ibid., p. 13, (original source: Julia and Herman Schwendinger, "Rape Myths: In Legal, Theoretical and Everyday Practice", 'Crime and Social Justice,' I, Spring-Summer, 1974).

90. Philip Agee, 'Inside The Company' (New York: Bantam Books,1975), p. 8.

91. 1bid., p. 9.

92. 1bid., p.64.

93. Ibid., p. 617.

94.'The Washington Post,' March 9,1976, 11,1, 'The San Francisco Examiner', March 9, 1976, 1,1.

95. David Wallechinsky and Irving Wallace, 'The People's Almanac', (New York: Doubleday & C0., Inc. 1975). p.52.

96. Op Cit., Fromm, (original Source: John Dewey, 'Freedom and Culture', C.P.Putman's Sons, New York, 1939).

97. Ibid., p.249.

98. Ibid., p. 253.

99. Ibid., p.255.

100. Ibid., p.256.

101. Ibid., p.246.

102. Ibid., p. 139.

103. Michael Glenn and Richard Kunnes, 'Repression or Revolution? Therapy in the U.S. Today', (New York: Harper Colophon Books, Harper and Row, 1973), pp. 46—7.

104.'The San Francisco Chronicle', June 16, 1977, 7,1.

105.'Madness Network News', (Madness Network News Inc., San Francisco, Vol. 4,#2) pp. 1-2.

106. Keneth Wooden, 'Weeping in the Playtime of Others' (New York: McGraw Hill Book Co., 1975), pp. 6—8, 12—13, 9, 78.

107. Op Cit., Glenn and Kunnes, P. 8.

108. Harvey Wasserman, "Pulling the Plug on Solar," New Age (vol. 3, Sept.1977), p. 46.

109. Ibid., p. 46.

110. 1bid., p. 49.

111. Gene Youngblood, "The Mass Media and the Future of Desire," 'The Co-Evolution Quarterly', (Issue 16, Winter, 1977-78) p. 12

112. Op Cit., Fromm, p. 119.

113. Ibid., p. 128.

114. Ibid., p. 168.

115.'Back to that Old-time Religion," 'Time', December 26, 1977, p. 53.

116. Chuck Fager, "Bill Bright's Evangelical Plan to Save America," 'The San Francisco Bay Guardian' May, 1977, p. 7.

117. Andrew Kopkind, "Grassroots Militancy," 'New Times' Oct., 1977,p.6.

118. Ibid., p.6.

119. Alan Crawford, "Richard Viguerie's, Bid for Power," 'The Nation', January 29, 1977, Vol. 244, #4, p. 105.

120. 1bid., p. 105.

121. 1bid., p. 105.

122. 1bid., p. 106.

123. Ibid., p 1O8.

124. Ibid., p. 108.

125. 1bid., p. 107.

126. Ibid., p. 104.

127. Ibid., p. 106.

128. 'The Washington Post', Sept. 6, 1977, 3, 2.

129. Ibid., 3, 2.

130. Walter R. Laguer, 'Young Germany'(New York: Basic Books, 1962), p.41-42.

www.ingramcontent.com/pod-product-compliance
Lightning Source LLC
Chambersburg PA
CBHW071119280326
41935CB00010B/1057